Communion
Services and Video Clips on DVD

Igniting Worship Series
Communion

Services and Video Clips on DVD

Grace Community Church & SpiritFilms™

Abingdon Press
Nashville, Tennessee

IGNITING WORSHIP SERIES: COMMUNION

© Copyright 2003 by Abingdon Press

All rights reserved.

This book is printed on acid-free, recycled paper.

ISBN 0-687-02588-5

Scripture quotations designated (NIV) are from the Holy Bible, New International Version copyright © 1973, 1978, 1984 by the International Bible Society. Used by permission of Zondervan Bible Publishers.

Adobe, the Adobe logo, Adobe Premiere, Adobe Photoshop, and Adobe Elements are trademarks of Adobe Systems Incorporated.

Microsoft, Microsoft Office, PowerPoint, and PowerPoint Viewer are registered trademarks of Microsoft Corporation.

Macintosh® and QuickTime® are registered trademarks of Apple Computer, Inc.

Other product and company names mentioned herein may be the trademarks of their respective owners.

04 05 06 07 08 09 10 11 12—10 9 8 7 6 5 4 3 2
MANUFACTURED IN THE UNITED STATES OF AMERICA

Contents

There's a Bug on the Bread

I had been appointed to my first church for about eight months. The fringes of springtime were emerging from winter respite. The bishop had called all of the newly appointed ministers to a retreat and was going to inspire us and send us into ministry. I didn't know what to expect but I got in my little Corolla and drove over to North Louisiana Conference Campground. It was a beautiful spring day. There were flowers coming up all over the place. Brown patches of grass were starting to turn green and the clover was beginning to bloom. The birds were singing and the sky was blue with just a few billowy clouds above. I pulled into the camp. Even though I am not originally from Louisiana, my father—who started his ministry here—had shown me this camp many years before. He had shared with me events that had happened at this and other camps around the state in past years. I began to recall these stories, and I felt connected to all this history. Coming here as a minister, however, was a new experience for me.

I met a group of ministers at the big, old lodge. We walked through the trees and sat in the amphitheater. The bishop started to speak and recounted how we were part of the ones who were called in the line of the apostles, the apostles who had been called by Jesus: "Come and follow me, and I'll make you fishers of men." At that moment, a small boat came into view on the lake right behind the bishop. It was as if the Board of Ordained Ministry had staged it, and the boat was coming into sight right on cue. "Wow! Look at that!" I thought to myself. He continued to talk about God's purposeful activity in creation and in the redemption of the world. On the edge of the amphitheater was a rough-hewn cross standing out against the clear blue sky. As we sat there surrounded by giant, towering pine trees, I became aware of how those trees stretched upward with their beautiful new foliage, taking in the sunlight and producing food and energy to sustain those branches and roots. At the same time, the roots grew down into the earth, pulling nourishment and water up from the soil. The sunlight shone in thin and wide shafts through the trees. I could feel the shafts of light shining on my legs, surrounding us with the warmth and life-giving energy of the sun. As I observed this, I became aware of the physics of light and the interaction of space and time and us. I felt the warmth of the sun and its life-giving energy.

Then the bishop began talking about the sacraments. A loaf of bread and a cup of wine were on the table behind him. I thought about the grapes and the vine and abiding in the vine. I thought about the crushing of the grapes and the process of making wine. I thought about the wine as the representation of the blood of Jesus that was poured out for our redemption. I thought about how the wheat came forth from the earth and about how it is made into flour. I thought about how leaven must be added so the dough can rise up and take its full shape. After it is baked, the bread comes forward and represents the body of Christ. That same process has been part of the Christian experience across thousands of years. Just then my thoughts were interrupted as a butterfly floated into our midst. It lightly danced on the soft breezes, passing through the shafts of shadow and light. Then it landed on the bread.

I was blown away. There, in the woods at an old Methodist camp on a spring day, I was having a religious experience of the convergence of story, time, the harmony of the physical processes of nature, tradition, symbolic action, and a living symbol of resurrection. *I saw it all at once. In that moment I understood. That was a moment where mystery and meaning opened up for me.* Experience, history, meaning, and symbol were layered and intertwined, and in that moment of convergence, they welled up inside of me and I could not contain myself. I turned to my friend sitting next to me and asked, "Oh my, did you see that?" "Yeah," he responded, "There's a bug on the bread."

Communion can be a powerful experience, and yet often it becomes a rote activity that we perform without seeing the miracles that are present. I remember the scene in "Our Town" when Emily returned to Grover's Corners after she died. She was awakened to a new awareness. She saw all of the moments of mundane life as jewels to be valued and savored. She saw life with deeper vision because she saw it in a different context and from a different perspective. *Similarly, I believe that sometimes it is helpful to look at our liturgical life together from different perspectives so we can maintain a fresh understanding of the truth and the mystery of God's grace.*

Liturgy is a powerful tool for the Church. It is the vehicle that conveys the heart of theology through acts of worship. Yet the liturgy is not ultimately the thing we strive to perpetuate and preserve. At the *heart* of the liturgy is the pearl of great price. There are times when we must experience the same pearl in different ways and from different perspectives in order to be awakened again to the depth, power, and simple complexity of the story. *This book is not about replacing or disrespecting the Church's order of worship; it is a book of services that provide some creative, alternative experiences.* Even though these services are not "traditional," they evoke an understanding of the meaning and spirit of the Christian year and the traditions of the Church. There are many ways to experience the powerful story of bread and cup.

HOW TO USE THIS RESOURCE

Included in this volume is a variety of worship services centered on the Sacrament of Holy Communion that make use of many different media forms and engage people from different ages and backgrounds to help retell the sacred story. A DVD containing a variety of resource clips and images accompanies this book. One set of clips gives insight into the way parts of the services were originally accomplished. The other set of clips has been created and provided by SpiritFilms™, an imprint of United Methodist Communications. These clips are designed to be multimedia resources for creative use in your own communion services. Some of the still images would be great backgrounds for the projection of liturgy or lyrics. The video clips might also be used as backdrops for a story being told during a sermon or children's time. The montage of communion images in different settings might become part of the liturgy on Maundy Thursday or World Communion Sunday. There is no "right way" to use video in worship. It is simply one more tool for the communication of the gospel that unites the believers and helps us focus on God.

USING MULTIMEDIA IN WORSHIP

Video and projected images can be used in a variety of ways in worship. Sometimes a clip from a movie makes a point in a powerful way that aids in the process of communication. Sometimes video allows for the sharing of an experience that adds depth to the experience of the worshiper. For example, on Ash Wednesday, as we were talking about the transience of life and the image of returning to ashes, we showed silent footage—without any additional commentary—of piles of rusted and junked cars projected on the screen above the table. The images clarified the message and added another level of truth without an extra word being spoken. On another occasion, we showed images of the children in the church kneading bread as the story of their class learning the meaning of communion was being told. A visual center in the worship space provides an area where the creative use of visual symbols can help people enter the particular dimension of God's story around which the service is focused. Four great resources that help explain the development of imagery in worship and leadership are *The Wired Church, Digital Storytellers, Out on the Edge,* and *Visual Leadership.*[1]

Various forms of visual media can be used to express the theme of each worship service. The Table, a visual center in the worship space, provides an area where the creative use of visual symbols can help people enter the particular dimension of God's story around which the service is focused.[2] The projection of digital images can also help the congregation begin to focus on the theme of the service as they enter the worship area. Often a main image, consisting of the theme or title of the service and the main visual metaphor, is used to provide a visual backdrop throughout the service when other images, lyrics, or liturgy are not being projected. Several examples of altar displays can be seen in the video clips provided on the DVD, as well as examples of thematic slides. Other forms of visual art, such as banners, oil paintings, fabric art, and children's art, may also be incorporated in the worship environment to enhance the theme.

THE PATTERNS & PROCESSES OF WORSHIP DEVELOPMENT

It is important as you look at these services to understand the context and setting in which they were created, not so that you can attempt to recreate them in exactly the same manner, but to help you more adequately modify them for your own situation. In developing the worship service, careful attention is given to building the experience around a central theme. Diverse elements are used in different orders to accomplish this task. While many services contain similar elements, the order is frequently different based on the most effective layering of expression and meaning to evoke congregational understanding and response. The gifts and input of several creative members of the congregation add to the richness of the worship development process.[3] Through these elements, doorways are provided for participants to enter the life-giving story of God's interaction with humanity.

The Gathering

As people arrive for services they are encouraged to participate in a time of music. These few minutes before the worship hour are used in a variety of ways. Singing familiar songs and hymns draws people into an attitude of worship. Instrumental jazz allows people a time of centering and focus as they prepare to worship. Teaching a new piece of music during this time for a couple of weeks allows the congregation to become familiar with "new liturgy" that will be used in upcoming services of worship.

Welcome and Community Connection

As the music ends, the worship leader encourages the congregation to participate in active hospitality by welcoming those around them and introducing themselves to someone new.[4] Then one of the pastors welcomes the congregation, welcomes first-time visitors, and makes announcements. Every attempt is made to keep this portion of the service brief. To keep the congregation focused, only those current events that affect the larger part of the gathered community are announced. Everyone is encouraged to read the bulletin, the prayer concerns, and any special inserts. Additional information about these items can be provided through sources such as scrolling announcements on TV monitors in the gathering area, an information center stocked with brochures, the newsletter, and the website.

Children's Time

The next element of the service, Children's Time, serves as the framework upon which the theme of the service begins to be built for the entire congregation. This is not a time in the service when adults are encouraged to fill out attendance registers. This part of the worship experience is relevant for the entire congregation.

It is very important to help children feel comfortable in the worship space. Although the whole worship experience is accessible to children, Children's Time provides a special time for them to learn an age appropriate truth connected with the theme of the service, and to learn to view their pastors as their friends.

On communion weekends, the children frequently participate in the sacrament during Children's Time, so that they know they are welcome at Communion. This way, those children leaving the service for other children's activities have the opportunity to receive communion, while others may stay in the service and participate in the sacrament again with their parents.

Opening Music

As the children leave for Sunday School or children's activities, the congregation is invited to come into God's presence with singing. The time of opening music "establishes that our worship is communion with God as well as with one another. They [prayers and praise] include recognition of who we are before God by centering on the nature and gifts of God" (*The United Methodist Book of Worship*, p. 20). Music used during this time becomes our call to worship and time of invocation and centering, the lyrics emphasizing the theme of the service. Only familiar songs and hymns are sung during opening music so that the congregation can sing and worship comfortably.

One major complaint about "contemporary" worship services is that the theology contained in the songs and hymns is shallow at best. Hundreds of song lyrics and musical styles are reviewed in order to ensure that the theology conveyed is meaningful and Wesleyan and the music is singable. This resource includes a wide variety of musical suggestions, many of which may be unfamiliar, but can become either a teaching opportunity to expand the musical database of your congregation or a place to substitute music that is more appropriate for your congregation. It is also important to remember that as time goes by, songwriters will produce new music that will also convey the themes of these services. Substituting such songs in the future will allow for this material to remain a viable resource for years to come. Hymn references given in the services are from *The United Methodist Hymnal* and are designated as **UMH**. However, most of the hymns suggested can also be found in a variety of other hymnals.

The Pastoral Prayer and The Lord's Prayer

The pastoral prayer incorporates intercession, confession, struggle, and thanksgiving, usually moving directly into the Lord's Prayer which is always printed in the bulletin, in case there is someone in attendance who is unfamiliar with it. The prayer is often followed by a song response: a verse of a traditional hymn, a *Taizé* piece, or a short chorus.

The Offering

Before the offering, the congregation is reminded that giving back a portion of that with which God has blessed them is an important and meaningful act of worship. Often included are a few words of intentional educational emphasis so that visitors might gain a healthy understanding of what this act of worship means. During the offering, a special piece of music, more congregational singing, or a "Ministry Moment" video vignette draws the congregation further into the focus of the service.

The Scripture

The Scripture reading is much more than simply the reading of the text. The pastor is careful to set the Scripture in its narrative context to help the congregation enter into the story. Drawing people into the circumstances surrounding the text allows for the Scriptures to come to life and take on new meaning in connection with the message for the particular theme of the service.

Sermon Summary

Each of the following worship experiences contains a portion of the sermon transcribed from the oral delivery. This form is utilized intentionally to provide a window into the visual style of communication used to proclaim God's Word or "to tell the story." More information can be found about this method of communication in *Visual Leadership: The Church Leader as ImageSmith* by Rob Weber (Abingdon Press, 2002).

Elements of Multisensory Engagement

Through the use of projection, drama, video, creative movement, special music, or other media, the congregation is engaged in a variety of ways that allow for a further unfolding of the story throughout the service. These elements are never incorporated just for the sake of incorporation; they are used in a service only when they directly impact or enhance the worship experience. Care is taken to avoid overuse of any one multisensory element and to ensure that it is incorporated in a quality manner.

Consecration of the Elements & Invitation to Holy Communion

As the service moves into the time of communion, the consecration of the elements is generally incorporated in the last portion of the sermon so that there is no break in the service flow. The people come forward, and Holy Communion is then received by intinction as a special piece of music is played or the congregation sings. If participation in communion in this particular way does not work with your situation, you can modify these services.

Prior to the distribution of the elements, an invitation is issued to extend *the hospitality of grace* and to open the door for people to *receive God's grace* as they participate in this sacrament.

In our denomination, the Communion table is an open table for all those desiring to draw closer to God through Jesus Christ: "All who intend to lead a Christian life, together with their children, are invited to receive the bread an cup. We have no tradition of refusing any who present themselves desiring to receive. Any or all of the people may receive them while standing, kneeling, or seated . . . . Every effort should be made to make each person, and especially children, welcome at the table." (*The United Methodist Book of Worship*, pp. 29–30). Remember, grace is available to all people—not just United Methodists—you simply must be willing to receive it. While most of the major Protestant denominations also believe in open communion, most qualify this invitation by emphasizing the need for individuals to be baptized prior to receiving Holy Communion. However, in our experience, we have seen many people enter into a relationship with God as they experienced communion who then requested baptism. The openness of the table allowed them to experience an acceptance they had not found before. It was that acceptance (like the prodigal son coming home) that opened the door to their acceptance of God.

The Invitation

The invitation is incorporated with the sending forth in a slightly different way each week. Not every service in this volume contains an Invitation and Sending Forth. You will want to tailor the Invitation for your particular setting. The following example illustrates how this invitation might be worded:

If there is anyone here who wants to find out more about what it means to share in the gift of life in a Christian community, learn more about your identity as a child of God, or give your life to the One who gives life to us, Jesus Christ, then I would invite you to come forward and meet with me after the service. I would love to visit with you and help you along that path. If anyone wants to become a member of this congregation of the United Methodist Church, I would love to talk with you about that, also. I can share with you what discipleship and church membership are, and how we can move together in that direction.

AN INVITATION TO IMAGINE

As you experience the services in this book, try not to look upon them with an overly analytical eye. Rather, allow yourself to see beyond the ink and paper into the creative possibility of your congregation experiencing the reality of God's grace in fresh ways. As you prayerfully enter these services and imagine what God may hold in store for you, it is our hope that along the way you may glimpse a vision of the miraculous beyond . . . so much more than a bug on the bread.

ENDNOTES

1. Michael Slaughter, *Out on the Edge* (Nashville: Abingdon Press, 1998); Len Wilson and Jason Moore, *The Wired Church* (Nashville: Abingdon Press, 1999) and *Digital Storytellers* (Nashville: Abingdon Press, 2002); Rob Weber, *Visual Leadership: The Church Leader as Image-Smith* (Nashville: Abingdon Press, 2002).

2. Learn more about altar design and training for altar teams at www.newwinedesign.com.

3. In our congregation, we have a group of creative minds called SPIN (Sharing, Planning, and Imagining on Neutral ground) who work to incorporate such elements as altars, art, drama, photography, video, music, creative movement, and hospitality in the theme of each week's service.

4. Igniting Ministry is a coordinated series of efforts by United Methodist Communications to assist local churches in strengthening their welcoming and media skills. This effort includes a national advertising campaign ("Open Hearts, Open Minds, Open Doors") to help raise awareness of the United Methodist Church. For more information, visit www.ignitingministry.org.

Service 1

Coming Home for Communion

Scripture: Psalm 27

Entering the Story

As Christians we find our home in the story of Christ's activity in the world. This Advent communion service focuses on the idea of Advent preparation as returning home to that story.

Service Connections

The altar is designed to resemble a dinner table. There are no knives, forks, or plates, but the candles and chalices make it appear as though a family feast is waiting. Only one candle is lit at the beginning of the service. There are twelve other candles on the table to be lighted toward the end of the service.

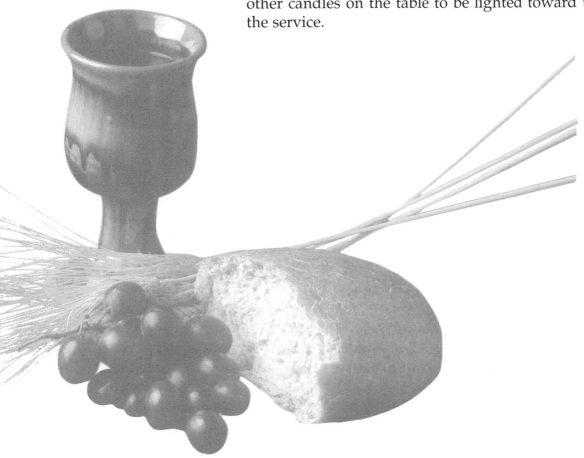

THE SERVICE

Welcome and Community Connection

Children's Time Suggestion

Have you ever been on a long trip? It may have been a wonderful trip, but there is still something about coming home that feels comfortable and good. You can put on your comfortable clothes or your pajamas and eat your favorite food from home that you can't buy at a restaurant. It feels good to come home.

Coming to the Communion Table for Christians is like coming home as well. When we come to the table we come to be with Jesus, who loves us and cares for us no matter where we have been. We don't have to dress up a certain way or pretend to be something we're not because he accepts us just as we are and invites us to share in the meal. Think about coming to Communion as coming home. No matter where you are, no matter where you go, no matter what you become in life, there will always be a place you can call home.

(The children are then served Communion.)

Opening Music

"Prepare the Way" by Darrell Evans and Eric Nuzum
©1999 Integrity's Hosanna! Music (c/o Integrity Music, Inc.)

The Pastoral Prayer and The Lord's Prayer

A Time of Explanation during the Advent Season

It is important to remember that if you are reaching out to the unchurched, there will be those who do not understand the ritual and tradition of your church. The Christian Year does not make sense to everyone who walks through your doors. Advent, Ash Wednesday, Lent, and Maundy Thursday are just a few examples of terms that are confusing. Unless we are intentional about incorporating explanation into our worship times, some may never understand the significance of these events and how they are connected with Christmas and Easter. You may have learned about the Christian Year in Sunday School or confirmation class. But if you are reaching beyond the walls of your immediate congregation, then you want to be sure to provide times when the seasons of the liturgical year are explained. An example of this type of "education" within the worship format is found in this Advent Communion service.

Advent may be a strange word for some. The season of Advent is the season of preparing for Christmas, getting ready for Christmas . . . waiting for Christmas. In our consumer society, we seem to skip Advent and roll into the Christmas season earlier and earlier to make more time for shopping. *In the Scripture, the themes of preparation, waiting, and not being sure of God's gift but trusting that God will provide are important.* Waiting in trust and uncertainty is what the season of Advent is about. Advent is about waiting, preparing, and being open to the promise of God that is yet to be fulfilled. One Advent tradition found in many churches is the use of the Advent wreath. It is not something that is found in Scripture, but neither are chairs, yet chairs serve a purpose. You sit in them. The wreath serves a purpose as well. It is a symbolic representation of what the season of Advent is all about. Let me take a moment to explain some of the symbolism found in the wreath. It can become more than just an ornament for us.

1) Notice that the wreath is in the shape of a circle, which is one of the purest geometric forms. A circle is the symbol of eternity. It is something that has no beginning and no end.

2) The wreath is made of evergreen, which is also a symbol of the eternal and a reminder of the gift of life that God has given us through Jesus Christ.

3) The wreath has candles on it, which can represent many things, and certainly that God is the light of the world for us. We do not light them all at once because we want to understand the preparation and waiting. You may have had one of those calendars as a child on which you open a door each day as you anticipate the coming of Christmas. Each day you open another door and find a message telling you something to do or giving you a piece of candy. This experience of waiting helped build excitement about the approach of Christmas. Likewise, we do not light the candles all at once. We light one each week until finally, on Christmas Eve, we light the Christ candle. It is a process of waiting and building anticipation.

Last night as I was waiting for the service to start I came into the worship area and noticed a mom leading her little child to the nativity. They seemed to be searching around the wreath and the manger for something. Then I heard the little child say, "Nope, he's not here yet," because the little infant Jesus was not in the manger. Advent is the season of waiting for that gift.

Scripture Reading: Psalm 27

(The Scripture is read and the Advent candle is lit.)

After the Scripture is read, these words become a moment of congregational response. Each line is read and the congregation is encouraged to repeat them.

The Lord is my light and my salvation.
Whom shall I fear?
The Lord is my light and my salvation.
Of whom shall I be afraid?

A Time of Offering

The congregation is led in singing "O Come, O Come Emmanuel" as the offering is received.

Pastoral Prayer of Preparation Example

God, thank you for your presence with us now. Help us to feel it. Thank you for the gifts that you give us. You give us air to breathe—air that moves through the beautiful leaves, causing them to whisper and to fall—and we are reminded of your touch at every stage of life.

God, you know that by myself I am not able or worthy do what you have called upon me to do, to share your words with this your gathered family. Yet you do call and so I cry out back to you, Lord, "Help. Be with me as I speak. Shape the words as they come forth from my mouth that they might be pleasing unto you." More importantly, God, breathe into this place now and stir our hearts, just as the wind whispers through the trees. Remove any barrier that would keep us from hearing what you would say to us no matter what is spoken. We know that you have that power. In the name of Jesus, we ask that you would speak. Let your servants be listening. Amen.

Sermon Summary

The beginning of this sermon walks the congregation through memories of home, a powerful image that shapes us and forms who we are. The congregation is asked to remember what "going home" means to them personally. Tell a personal story of the wonderful memories of home to help set the framework for home as a place of comfort and peace. Juxtapose this image with a story of a homeless man and his dog eating out of a dumpster, thus identifying the image of home as one that may not always be pleasant. Once various images of what home might be are established, the words of David are examined for a clearer understanding of where home can truly be found:

Where is home? In verse four of Psalm 27, I think David has the key for us: *"One thing I ask the Lord, this is what I seek. That I may dwell in the house of the Lord all the days of my life."* Now some people might read this and say, "Okay, we are going to live for eternity in the house of the

Lord." While that's great (living for eternity with God), David wants us to remember that no matter where he finds himself (in cave, in palace, at peace, at war), he can dwell in the house of the Lord each and every day. Our home is not found in our memory, or in a place, or in a person, or in stuff, but in God. As Augustine said, "Our hearts are restless until they find their rest in Thee."

Remember that song, "He's Got the Whole World in His Hands"? It's true. God holds this whole world and each life in his hand. Sometimes that is easy to see, and we are so aware that God is in control. We can see the amazing power of God's creation in the beauty of the sunset or the trees.

There's a story of a pastor who looked out his window and saw a kitten in a tree. So he went out and tried to coax the kitten out of the tree. When calling the kitten didn't work, he decided to get a can of tuna. He put the tuna at the base of the tree and went back inside and watched. The cat still did not move. Next, he put out milk but that didn't work either. So he got a rope and tied one end around the young tree and the other end to the bumper of his car. Very slowly he backed the car up, bending the tree in hopes that the limb would come down far enough for him to reach the cat. "Just a little farther," he thought; but he had pulled it too far. The rope broke and the cat flew into the air. He was horrified. He had no idea where the cat had gone. He felt sure he had killed it.

A few days later he saw a woman from his church at the store. She was buying cat food. He knew that she hated cats so he inquired why she was buying cat food. She replied, "You won't believe this," and told him how her little girl had been begging her for a cat, but she had refused. Then a few days before, when the child had begged again, she finally told her little girl, "Well, if God gives you a cat, I'll let you keep it." She told the pastor, "I watched my child go out in the yard, get on her knees, and ask God for a cat. And really, Pastor, you won't believe this, but I saw it with my own eyes. A kitten suddenly came flying out of the blue sky, with its paws spread out, and landed right in front of her." The girl kept the cat.

Although we do not see things like that very often, we can be assured that God IS in control of life, that the whole world is in God's hands. Sometimes it's easy to see, but sometimes it's not as easy to see. Think about Joseph and Mary. The whole trip to Bethlehem would have been bad enough in a car, much less on a donkey. And when they arrive, there's no place for them to stay except a humble stable. The mother of the child of God can't even get a room? Is God really in control?

Maybe some of you have had a similar experience. You feel alone. Or your disease kicked back in or someone that you loved left or passed away. Your life doesn't feel like blessings are falling out of the sky into your lap. But Joseph and Mary, even in that difficult situation, didn't give up hope; they kept going. They held on to the words of David, who in the midst of his struggle said, "I'm still confident of this. I will see the goodness of the Lord in the land of the living. Wait for the Lord. Be strong. Take heart. And wait."

The season of Advent is about *waiting* for Christ's coming, not simply a month-long celebration of his coming. We learn that even in this waiting time, even in that time when the promises don't seem to be fulfilled, even in the midst of our struggles, God is in control. So during this season, we will be taking a series of journeys home—home into the presence of, the reality of, and the gifts of God. We will remember that underneath the welcome mat, just outside the stable in Bethlehem, we can find the key to the home that will never be sold, will never go away, will never be destroyed. We will find our home in the story of the incarnation of God.

Again the congregation is encouraged to repeat these words:

> **The Lord is my light and my salvation.**
> **Whom shall I fear?**
> **The Lord is my light and my salvation.**
> **Of whom shall I be afraid?**

A Time of Prayer and Transition into Multisensory Engagement

(The lights slowly fade to black during the following prayer.)

Lord, I do not know what is going on in the lives of each of these your children today, but you do. I don't know whether they are happy and have homes filled with joy, whether they hurt or feel alone, or whether they have been far away and are turning back now, hoping that there might be a candle flickering on the porch to welcome them. I don't know, God, but you do. You call each of us to find our home not in the things of this world—no matter what the situation—but rather in you. Amen.

Song: "Home Tonight" by Chris Rice
©2000 Clumsy Fly Music (Adm. by Word Music, Inc.)

As the song begins, lights come up on the soloist while the only other light comes from a lighted single candle on the altar. As the song moves into the first chorus, have a youth light the other twelve candles. As the song ends, the lights come up and the pastor is seated beside the altar/communion table.

A video clip illustrating this can be found on the DVD that accompanies this book. Go to the "Video Clips" section, then choose "Illustrative Clips," and select the clips for "Coming Home for Communion."

Consecration of the Elements

In the Old Testament, the altar was the resting place, the dwelling place of God, where people came to offer sacrifices. In the New Testament, the center of the Christian community became the table. There's something about the table. Something about coming home and gathering around the table with the ones that you love and sharing nourishment, story, memory, and love. Maybe that's why Jesus chose *(unwrapping the bread)* the table to be the place of the sacrament of richest memory, a place where we come together as a family at God's table and break bread and remember what he did. Jesus said, "This is My Body, given for you." *(After the bread is broken, it is placed back on the altar and the chalice and pitcher are lifted.)* Maybe he chose the table because it was there that people would gather and share joy, and laughter, and song. So when he poured the wine and said, "This is the cup of the new covenant for you and for many, for the forgiveness of sins," he attached that memory to the table. "Every time you eat this bread and drink this cup, remember Me." *(After pouring, the pitcher and cup are placed back on the altar.)*

As you come forward to the table, do not think about coming to some altar where you have to offer a sacrifice. Instead, think about coming home to the dinner table that God has set for you. A table where you are welcome, no matter where you have been, what you've been through, or what your situation in life is. As long as you want to draw closer to God through Jesus Christ and you are willing to say, "God, where am I far from you; where have I sinned? Forgive me," then there is a place for you.

(Communion servers are asked to come forward.)

O God, pour out your Spirit upon each one of us, and upon these gifts of bread and wine. Help them be for us the body and the blood of our Lord, Jesus Christ, that we might be his Body in the world. Help us find a place at your table and know that no matter what our situation, we are home in you. Amen.

Holy Communion

Instrumental music begins moving into a time of singing. Two effective songs to use would be: "Come, Thou Long Expected Jesus" (UMH 360) and "My Heart, Your Home" by Christy and Nathan Nockels.

©1997 Rocketown Music (Admin. by Word Music Group, Inc.), Word Music, Inc. (a div. of Word Music Group, Inc.), and Sweater Weather Music (Admin. by Word Music Group, Inc.)

(As Communion is completed, the congregation is invited to stand and sing as "My Heart, Your Home" comes to a close.)

The Invitation and Sending Forth

(*After Communion is served and the congregation has returned to their seats, the pastor stands and speaks.*)

When things aren't going right and you've "flung the cat"—whatever that might be for you—learn to stop and say wherever you are, "Into your hands I commit my life." There you will find home. Try it.

Congregation says these words together: "Into your hands I commit my life."

Invitation

As we go forth from this place, remember that every day you dwell in the house of the Lord. Go in peace. Amen.

Service 2

Communion on Christmas Eve

Scripture: Luke 2:8–20

Entering the Story

God became human so that humanity could come face to face with incarnate love. We gather because we are ones who, in one way or another, have been touched by that same God. With this understanding, it is up to us to take on the role of being the hands and feet of Christ, the light of Christ in the world, so that all might know of this love and grace.

Service Connections

One of the most important connecting elements for the Christmas Eve service revolves around creating an atmosphere of "helpfulness" for visitors. Your hosts, ushers, and greeters play a vital role in helping people experience God. Though they are always an important part of any worship experience, when there are many visitors, the hosts' help and direction provides newcomers with a sense of welcome and peace. Where are the restrooms? Where is the nursery? Where can I find out more information about this church? Typically, Christmas Eve services are very full, and finding the correct number of seats for a family may provide a sense of comfort that allows them to experience God that evening. Providing a child with a worship coloring packet (a simple plastic bag with crayons and a color sheet which connects to the theme of the service) helps a parent to know his or her family is welcomed and cared for. All of these hospitable acts are crucial to keeping the "open hearts, open minds, and open doors" attitude evident.

The Gathering

Instrumental arrangements of favorite seasonal hymns are often effective for this time of gathering. Christmas Eve is a hectic time as parents rush in from the mall, visitors wander in who are not familiar with the facility or the service, and restless children eagerly await Christmas Day. Instrumental music can help serve as a time of centering. Starting five minutes late is often helpful on Christmas Eve.

THE SERVICE

Welcome and Community Connection

Opening Music

Play a combination of seasonal hymns or songs for congregational singing.

Children's Time

A retelling of the Christmas Story during this time creates a framework for the entire congregation's worship experience.

The Offering

Use a seasonal hymn or song for congregational singing.

Scripture Reading: Luke 2: 8–20

A Time of Explanation

During times when visitors increase, it is even more important to be sensitive to their incorporation into the service. Regarding communion, an explanation is given to visitors that the United Methodist communion table is an open table for those desiring to draw closer to God through Jesus Christ and those willing to ask, "Where am I far from You?" Remind the congregation that Christ is a savior to all the people, not just United Methodists.

If the congregation will light candles at the end of the service, it is helpful to explain how this will be done in advance. It is often difficult for children to deal with dripping wax, even when paper or plastic are added to the bottom of the candles. An excellent alternative for children is the use of white glow sticks, which are opened at the same time the adults are lighting their candles. The children love using glow sticks, and they are less stressful for parents.

If carried out correctly, this explanation will move people into the next part of the service knowing they will be welcome to participate in the acts of worship yet to come.

Pastoral Prayer of Preparation Example

God, we thank you that you have drawn us here. We are thankful for our lives even though they are sometimes filled with hectic distractions, chaos, emergencies, disappointments, and inconveniences. Yet these are all a part of the life you've graciously given us. Thank you for giving us life and caring enough for us to stay intimately involved in our lives, in our world, and throughout history. You sent your Child to be our Savior, to show us the depth and extent of your love. Part the veil of space and time and help us to glimpse you in this moment, to hear in the voice of a baby the voice of God, and to give thanks. So come, Jesus, and speak. Amen.

Sermon Summary

The sermon for the evening is based upon a story sent to me by a friend, via email, that gives us a glimpse into why we come together on an evening like Christmas Eve. It tells why God came into the world in the first place.

On one particular evening, in the midst of a snowstorm, a family was gathered to make the final preparations for Christmas evening. As Christmas music and the fragrance of hot cider filled the air, the last of the packages were wrapped. The time soon came to go to the Christmas Eve service, and the wife said to the husband, "Honey, are you coming with us to the Christmas Eve service?" and he said, "No, I'm not going to the Christmas Eve service." "We'd really like you to," said the wife. "We'd like to go as a family." "No," said the husband. "I don't want to go to the Christmas Eve service because I think I can find God here. That whole story just doesn't make much sense to me. The idea that God—awesome, creative, all-powerful God—would enter into the world as a child and then die seems ridiculous and incomprehensible. Why would God do that? Go ahead, I know they are always short on seats, so I'll give mine up. That will be my holiday sacrifice."

He tried to make light of it, but the family was not pleased. However, they did not want to stir things up too much, so they decided to go on without him. They went to the service where the music played, the candles glowed, and communion was served. Back at the house the man sat by himself, tending the fire. He walked over to look out the window at the moonlight shining down on the freshly fallen snow. Just outside his house, he saw a flock of birds that had been lost in the snow. He thought, "Those little tiny things don't have anything to eat as everything is covered with snow." He decided he would go out and take them some crumbs to eat. But when he went outside he scared them, and they flew away. Then he opened the door to the barn and turned the light on, hoping they would go inside and find warmth there. Waving his arms and moving toward the barn, he even tried to herd them inside, but instead he only drove them farther away. (It is rather hard to herd birds.)

He went back inside, trying to figure out how to get them into the barn. Then he thought, "If I could be a bird for just one moment, I could go into that barn and tell them where the warmth was and where they'd be able to stay safe from the storm!" Then, at that moment, he realized why it was that God—awesome, creative, all-powerful God—had become human. God became human to give us direction, to show us the place where we could gather in warmth and safety from the storm. The One who looked from beyond and saw us in the midst of our struggle and said, "Because I care for them, I will become one of them, share their frailty and their struggle, so that I can touch, and speak, and teach, and heal, and ultimately give myself that they might have life." This is the One, who was born in a simple manger and came to be with us.

We gather here as those who have been touched, in one way or another, by that same God. The one who created us, the one who sent Christ to redeem us, and the one who lives on to sustain us—the one who came as a child.

Consecration of the Elements

During your holiday preparations, you've brought out all of your decorations from the attic or basement or garage. Imagine unwrapping the pieces of the special ceramic nativity set given to you by a loved one, only to discover that baby Jesus' arm has somehow been broken. Though you are at first heartbroken that this treasure seems to be ruined, you realize that this broken figurine symbolizes an important truth: we are his hands now because Christ dwells in this world through us. *(Taking the bread)* And so that same One who came down to share with us love and life, to nourish our bodies and souls, sat at a table with his disciples and took bread, and said, "This is my Body which is broken for you." *(Taking the cup and pitcher)* He took the cup and thanked God, saying, "This is the cup of the new covenant poured out for you and for many for the forgiveness of sins. Every time you eat this bread and drink this cup, remember me." And so it is in these gifts of bread and cup that we are reminded of the one who came to be with us, the one who comes to dwell in us, and the one who comes to dwell through us.

God, pour out your Spirit upon each one of us and upon these gifts of bread and of cup. Help them be for us the Body and the Blood of our Lord, Jesus Christ, that we might be his body and his hands in this world, redeemed and active. Thank you once again that you have come to be with us and to show us life. Help us feast at the table that you have prepared, so that our lives may be nourished, for we do ask it in Jesus' name. Amen.

Holy Communion

During this time, instrumental hymns of the season may be played, or the congregation might be led in the singing of hymns as they participate in Communion.

A Transition to a Time of Multisensory Engagement

In those days as people sat in darkness, waiting and wondering, they cried out, "God, how long?" Into their darkness, God sent a great Light, a Light that has become our Light. And this Light will never be overcome by darkness. We celebrate the miracle of the coming of the Light of Christ into the world.

(Lights fade to black for special music, dance, and lighting of candles.)

"Light a Candle" by Joel Lindsay and Wayne Haun
  As recorded by Avalon ©1999 Paragon Music Corp. (ASCAP), Vacation Boy Music (ASCAP),
  both administered by Brentwood-Benson Music Publishing, Inc. and Christina Taylor Music
  (administered by Daywind Music Publishing)

If you have a liturgical dance team, this would be a wonderful opportunity for them to prepare an interpretation of the coming of the Light of Christ into the world. The dancers participate in creative movement through worship by combining the dance training they have received and their understanding of the message to be conveyed. Dance provides yet another point of interaction for the congregation to enter into the story and experience God.

If dancers are not available in your particular situation, this song can still be used as a time of special music when children or youth would come forward to finish the lighting of the candles on the altar and across the front of the worship area.

A Transition to the Lighting of the Congregational Candles

(The pastor receives light from the candle of one who has participated in the lighting of the candles on the altar.)

"As one candle is lit from another, the light is not diminished but increases. So it is with the light of Christ in each of you. As you give it away, it only grows."

(The light is passed from person to person as "Silent Night" begins. It is effective to sing the first verse again unaccompanied when the entire congregation has shared in the passing of the light.)

Sending Forth

For to you this day is born a Savior who is Christ the Lord. May God's peace fill you. May God's love overflow from your life and may you be a light to those in darkness. With God's Spirit and God's peace, know that you are God's hands in the world. Go in peace. Amen.

Service 3

Finding Refuge in Communion

Scripture: Psalm 5

Entering the Story

Finding refuge in God means finding a place of safety, a place of stability, and a place of comfort—not a place to hide. Refuge is a place where we can live out of God's fullness.

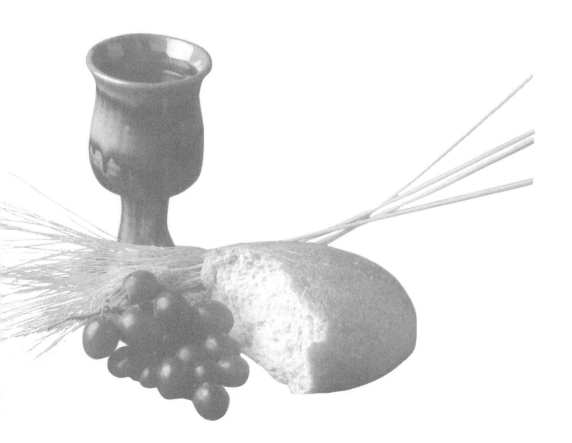

THE SERVICE

Welcome and Community Connection

Children's Time Suggestion

Set up a free-standing camping tent in the front of the sanctuary. When the children are invited forward for children's time, have them enter the tent with the pastor or leader. Tell them a story about camping in the rain and the way in which the tent offered protection from the storm. Remind the children of God's protection. Tell them that though God doesn't stop bad things from happening around them, God's protection will provide them a place to feel safe and surrounded by God's love.

Opening Music

"Jesus, Jesus" by Geoff Bullock
©1995 Word Music, Inc. (Admin. by Word Music Group, Inc.) and Maranatha! Music (Admin. by The Copyright Company)

"And That My Soul Knows Very Well" by Darlene Zschech
©1996 Darlene Zschech (Hillsong), Admin. in U.S. & Canada by Integrity's Hosanna! Music, and Russell Fragar (Hillsong), Admin. in U.S. and Canada by Integrity's Hosanna! Music

The Pastoral Prayer and The Lord's Prayer

The Offering

"Shield About Me" by Donn Thomas and Charles Williams
©1980 Spoone Music (Admin. by Word Music Group, Inc.) and Word Music, Inc. (a div. of Word Music Group, Inc.)

Scripture Reading: Psalm 5:1, 2, 3, 7, 8, 11, 12

I will read to you a passage of Scripture today that comes from the fifth Psalm, looking specifically at the way David finds refuge in God.

Pastoral Prayer of Preparation Example

Lord God, we thank you for giving us the opportunity to gather together this morning. We stand before you this morning as people seeking refuge and protection from the storms of life. Shelter us with your loving presence, giving us strength and assurance to live as faithful disciples.

God, I stand here this morning, knowing that in and of myself, I am not able or worthy to do what you've called me to do, but you've called, and so I'm here. I call back to you and ask for help. Be with me as I speak. Shape the words that come forth from my mouth, that they might be pleasing unto you. More importantly, touch each of us, so that no matter what is spoken, we might hear you. For we ask in Jesus' name, Amen.

Sermon Summary

As we begin today, I want you to think about a situation in your own life. Remember a time when you were afraid. Maybe you were alone. Maybe you were lost. Maybe you felt pursued or persecuted. Now remember where you sought refuge. Where was it that you found safety, or peace, or comfort?

Not long ago a man shared with me a powerful story about finding refuge. A walk through his old neighborhood had awakened in him this memory. He told of a child who had been playing along the street in a particular neighborhood. Someone pulled up and said, "Can you give me directions?" When the child got close enough, the man pulled the child into the car. The child was never seen again. This memory came to the man as he was walking along the street filled with beautiful houses. It was a nice neighborhood. Many nice people lived there. "How could this kind of thing happen?" he wondered. Then he noticed something he had not seen before. In one of the windows he saw a square, orange, fluorescent sign. It did not seem to fit on the front of one of those beautiful houses with nice landscaping. "Why is that orange sign there?" he wondered. He then looked a little closer and noticed there was an outline of a hand. He thought, "What is that?" He looked closer and saw the word *Refuge*. As he walked down the block he noticed these orange signs in several of the windows throughout the neighborhood.

The man discovered later that the people who lived in that neighborhood realized they had to do something to ensure that such an incident never occurred again. They banded together to form "safe" houses. They told all the children in the area: "If ever you have a problem, or you are lost, or you are being pursued, you can run to any house with an orange sign. There you'll find safety and someone who cares about you." These "safe" houses offered a true place of refuge.

When you are scared, when you are fleeing, or when you feel disconnected, where do you turn for refuge? Where do you turn for peace? I think we know the "right" answer. After all, we are the ones sitting here in church. We know the right answer is Jesus, that in him do we find refuge, forgiveness, hope, and a path directly to God. If we know this, why do we so frequently live a life of uncertainty and "peacelessness"?

We try to find refuge and certainty ourselves, to calm our fears and quiet our anxieties, not in Jesus, but in tangible things of this world. One of the ways we do this is to excel at what we do, to succeed, so that we are valued. If people value you, then you feel like you have a certain amount of stability. Or we believe that making enough money will provide us with refuge, with financial stability. Or we desperately try to get others to love us and need us. In that relationship of co-dependence, we have a certain sense of refuge because we believe we won't fail as long as we are loved and needed. Or we talk about others and how bad they are so that we can feel good about ourselves, and therefore build a certain kind of refuge. Some people look for refuge in different types of drugs or mind-altering substances. It is a fleeting kind of refuge, but it is something a person believes he or she can control. We look for refuge in many different ways. While we may manage to find some temporary escape or diversion, we will find true refuge only in God.

Even when we do seek the true source of our refuge in the right place, even when we try to draw near to God, we may still experience a lack of peace. Coming to God does not always mean that things will turn out well for us. We will still experience pain and sorrow and fear. The model that David presents for us is of one who nevertheless goes to God in expectation; in recognition and confidence that God is his true source of trust and safety. David prays to God every morning in the midst of his distress. People are saying false things about him. Others are pursuing him. Though he feels surrounded by enemies, David can still say with assurance: "Oh, Lord in the morning you hear my voice, in the morning I plead my case with you, and watch." This paints a picture of a person who gets up in the morning and meets with God. He lays his requests before God in the absolute faith that God hears his voice and waits expectantly and confidently for God to do something.

Notice that David does not say he waits for his requests to be granted. Instead, he says he waits with expectation, that God will actually move in his life. I'm here . . . and I'm waiting. What will you do in me?

The second one is this: "But I, through the abundance of your steadfast love, will enter your house, I will bow down toward your holy temple in awe of you." David knows that it is not because of his success or his power or his wealth or popularity that he will find refuge. Only through God's mercy and steadfast love will he find refuge and peace in the House of God. David knows that he is broken and hurting. He knows that it is only through the grace of God that he can enter into God's refuge.

Think about the picture of David's approach to God—one who comes in the morning expectantly listening for what God might really do in his life. In realization of his own brokenness and spiritual poverty, he comes in reverence and in the knowledge of the depth of God's love, kneeling at the feet of the Holy One who created all there is.

As we begin a new year, I want to invite you to look at how you approach holiness and your relationship with Jesus Christ the Savior. I want to ask you, to invite you, into a deeper place, close to the heart of God—a place at the Table. Coming to this place takes a little more preparation, a little more vulnerability, a little more sharing, and a little more willingness to see one another. Together we can find a place of refuge around this Table.

Consecration of the Elements

Where is it that you touch holiness? How is it that you approach holiness? I invite you this year to come and take your place at the festival table. You could see just the outline of a loaf of bread, or you could see a physical form, which frames the sacrifice of Jesus Christ. You could pick up this cup and approach it as if it were a cup that held tea or orange juice or you could see with eyes that allow you to know that it is a cup that represents covenant between you and God, containing not juice, but the very Blood of the Son of the Creator.

As we prepare today to come forward and share in these gifts of bread and cup, I invite you to shape your approach—to prepare yourself, to open yourself, and to drink deeply the presence of the Living God.

God, pour out your Spirit upon each one of us, and on these gifts of bread and wine. Help them be for us the Body and Blood of our Lord Jesus Christ. Help us to see with eyes that bypass normal, physical reality, and glimpse the presence of holiness. Help us see with your eyes those places in our hearts that are far from you, that distance us from you. Help us see where we are sinful. Help us to ask forgiveness with the knowledge that you will forgive. God, draw near to us, and help us in response to draw near to you.

Holy Communion

"You Bless Me Lord" by Scott Underwood
©1997 Mercy/Vineyard Publishing (Admin. by Music Services).

A Time of Musical Response

How many of you remember the words to the hymn, "Rock of Ages, cleft for me, let me hide myself in Thee"? This is not a desire to be in a place where one is hidden away from the world, but rather a place of shelter out of which we can grow. Like a seed that finds its hiding place in the soil, so we find our hiding place in God.

To close, I would like for us to lift those words up as a prayer. Lift up these words, approaching God with that same depth. Press in, draw near, and know that God is here for you.

Have the congregation sing "Rock of Ages, Cleft For Me"(UMH 361). You may also wish to arrange the chorus of "I Hide Myself in Thee" by Tommy Walker [©2000 Integrity's Praise! Music (c/o Integrity Music, Inc.)] with this traditional hymn.

The Invitation and Sending Forth

And so, hidden in the heart of God, *grow* in peace. Amen.

Service 4

Taking *in* Communion

Scripture: John 15:1–5

Entering the Story

In the act of "taking in" the body and blood of Christ it becomes part of who we are. We are nourished in symbol and truth by the elements. In this sacrament we realize that Christ's presence can never be taken away from us.

Service Connections

The video clip used in this service comes from the movie, *Phenomenon*, and can be located at 1:44:35–1:47:05, with the counter zero point set at the Touchstone Pictures title screen.

To show this clip, you must follow the appropriate copyright guidelines. More information can be found regarding motion picture licenses by visiting the Motion Picture Licensing Corporation website at www.MPLC.com or MPLC's new sister company, Christian Video Licensing International at www.CVLI.com.

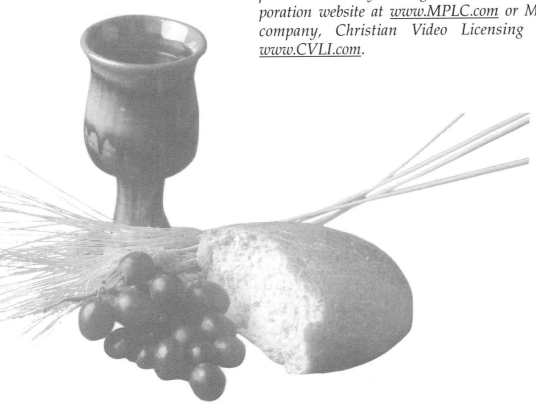

THE SERVICE

Welcome and Community Connection

Children's Time Suggestion

Provide small clay pots filled with potting soil and a packet of seeds for each child.

Ask the children, "If I leave these dried seeds in the packet, what will happen to them?" (*Nothing, they won't grow, they will stay the same.*) "If I want them to grow and live what will I have to do?" (*Plant them.*) That's right, you have to plant them in order for them to come to life. The same thing is true in our relationship with Jesus. If we let him stay distant—someone we only hear about at church—then our relationship won't grow. But if we take him inside and ask him to live in us, then a whole new life will begin to grow.

Give the children the pots and seeds to take home and plant. As the seed grows and as they care for the plant, they can think about their growing relationship with Jesus.

Opening Music

"Breathe on Me, Breath of God" (UMH 420)

"Breathe on Me" by Lucy Fisher
©1998 Lucy Fisher (Hillsong), Admin. in U.S. & Canada by Integrity's Hosanna! Music

The Pastoral Prayer and The Lord's Prayer

The Offering

"Be the Centre" by Michael Frye
©1999 Vineyard Songs (UK/Eire), Admin. by Music Services

Pastoral Prayer of Preparation

Sermon Summary

I once spoke with a rabbi who had visited a Christian church and observed the congregation participating in the sacrament of communion. He shared his impressions of this symbolic activity of the embodied sacrifice of God. He said, "What a beautiful experience. The symbols were so alive and powerful. I found myself wishing that we had something like this in our tradition—an act of taking God inside of us and nourishing us. I was almost in tears. As I continued to watch, however, I noticed that those sharing in the activity were doing so with blankness in their eyes. It seemed as if they were not aware of the blessing and beauty of the act in which they were participating. If only we had such an activity." Through the eyes of this rabbi, I was awakened again to the beauty and intricacy of the Sacrament of Holy Communion.

After this introduction, play the clip from the movie Phenomenon *and invite the congregation to consider the act of taking communion with new eyes. The clip contains a discussion between John Travolta's character, George Malley, and two children who live on the farm where he is staying. The children have come to realize that he is dying. They are upset because they don't want to feel abandoned again, as they did when their father left them. The young boy asks, "You came here to die, didn't you?" George holds an apple before them and explains that if it is left on the ground, the apple will decompose and disappear. If, however, one takes it inside oneself and eats it, then the apple becomes part of that person. It becomes something that can never be taken away. The children look at him deeply and then both passionately bite the apple. This clip became the bridge to enter the experience of communion. The comparison was drawn between simply "observing" the sacrament and actually "taking in" the Body and the Blood of Christ.*

Consecration of the Elements

Use "The Service of Word and Table V" from *The United Methodist Book of Worship* or a Communion liturgy from your denominational book of worship.

Holy Communion

"The Last Supper" by Cindy Morgan and Wes King
©1998 Sparrow Song (a div. of EMI Christian Music Publishing), Uncle Ivan Music (Admin. by EMI Christian Music Publishing), Word Music, Inc. (a div. of Word Music Group, Inc.)

Closing Music

"I Give You My Heart" by Reuben Morgan
©1995 Reuben Morgan (Hillsong), Admin. in U.S. and Canada by Integrity's Hosanna! Music

The Invitation and Sending Forth

Service 5

Creating Community in Communion

Scripture: Luke 6:27–31

Entering the Story

We come to the table to create community; to join together; to be blessed, healed, touched, cared for, strengthened, challenged, and oriented toward God. We are also called to share the forgiveness, given first to us by God, with one another.

Service Connections

The altar created for this particular service was a series of stepping stones that led to the foot of the cross. The table for the Communion elements was the last step at the base of the cross. Different colored scraps of leather were used to cover the cross, providing a visual symbol of and celebration of diversity. This table area became an example of the power of visual imagery to communicate the story of God in worship.

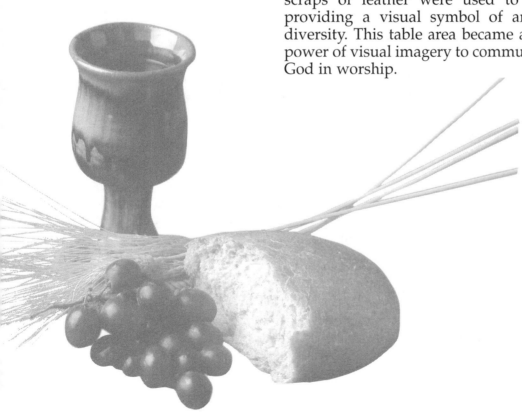

THE SERVICE

Welcome and Community Connection

Children's Time Suggestion

Tell a story about finding a puppy (and perhaps even bring one in for children's time) that was very sick and needed serious care from the vet. A great deal of money had to be spent to help the puppy get well. The puppy is now healthy, growing, and happy. (If you have an actual puppy, the children will be very attracted to it.) Now tell the children how the mission of Christians is much like caring for the puppy. Just as Jesus loves us when we make mistakes and seem unlovable, God wants us to care for others who might seem unlovable to us. This might be someone on the playground who no one else likes. It might be someone who has moved to town from another country and doesn't know the language. Or it might be a friend or family member who has made you angry or sad. But Jesus calls us to forgive as he has forgiven and love as he has loved.

Opening Music

"I Could Sing of Your Love Forever" by Martin Smith
©1994 Curious? Music UK (Admin. by EMI Christian Music Publishing)

"My Jesus, I Love Thee" (UMH 17)

In addition to the version found in The United Methodist Hymnal, *it is also effective to use the arrangement of this song found on Amy Grant's album "Legacy . . . Hymns & Faith" published by Word Music.*

The Pastoral Prayer and The Lord's Prayer

Scripture Reading: Luke 6:27–38

In the section before this passage from Luke, we find the beatitudes. Jesus had a way of turning ordinary stories, ordinary sayings, and ordinary wisdom upside down, and of making us see things in new and surprising ways. For instance, take the saying, "Blessed are the poor." We do not normally think of the poor as "blessed." Jesus takes things, flips them over, and twists our world around a bit.

He goes on to talk about loving your enemies and praying for those who persecute you. Then suddenly, in verse 37, Jesus says, "Do not judge and you will not be judged. Do not condemn and you will not be condemned. Forgive and you will be forgiven."

The song that you are about to hear has some words and images in it that turn our normal perspective on life upside down. "Turn up" your imagining and listen to the words of the song. God will bless us as we enter into this time of offering.

The Offering

"The Face of Christ" by Chris Rice
©2000 Clumsy Fly Music (Admin. by Word Music, Inc.)

Pastoral Prayer of Preparation Example

God, sometimes we see the face of Christ in the pictures in our Bible. Sometimes we see the face of Christ looking down from the cross. Sometimes we see the face of Christ in a caring teacher. Sometimes we see the face of Christ in a homeless person. You reach into our lives and take us and make us aware of something that is not what we usually think. So I say, "Lord, come on. I want to see."

God, I know that by myself, I am not able or worthy to do what you have called upon me to do, to share your words with this your family, and yet you have called and I am here. I call back asking, "help." Be with me as I speak. Shape the words as they come forth from my mouth that they might please you. More importantly, reach into this space and time now, and touch each ear, heart, mind, and spirit. Remove any barrier and help us to hear what you would have us hear, no matter what is spoken. We ask all this in Jesus' name. Amen.

Sermon Summary

We have come together as a diverse people. We've come from different places and have different histories, backgrounds, and memories. We have different educational levels, different jobs, and different experiences. We've come here for a variety of reasons; some of us have a clear vision of why we are here, some of us know only that we're looking for something that's missing from our lives. Yet we have all come together and we are sitting here in this room. What are we doing here? We are doing what Christians have done for a couple of thousand years—coming together in the name of Jesus Christ to form community, to knit community together, to be reminded of who we are as children of God, and to be focused on the One who created us. This is what we do when we gather. We come to be shaped as the people of God—formed, and healed, and touched, and strengthened, and encouraged, and challenged to be the people of God. We come to be oriented toward God, to become open and responsive to God's calling for our lives.

I think it's safe to say that not one of you has shared every single experience of the person sitting next to you. We are separate beings, separate entities, yet there is something that unites us. It is true that God's presence unites us here, but I want to look at this more specifically. What is it that is common to each one of us that unites us? God's grace. Why is that? God's grace is surrounding you, reaching out to you, leading you, comforting you, touching you, preparing you, protecting you, and offering you hope. Grace is there before you even respond, surrounding you.

There are some who come and have that experience of God's grace, that unconditional, unmerited, nothing-we-can-do-to-earn-it, gift of forgiveness. For those of you who have yet to experience this, it is there for the asking. Not one person in this world is beyond the reach of God's grace, though this may be hard to imagine at times. If Osama Bin Laden repented and begged forgiveness of God, he would be forgiven. God's grace is that strong. That doesn't say anything about the way I feel about Osama Bin Laden, but it says a great deal about how I understand the power of God's grace. I picked Osama because we all have a hard time with his actions. Our logic, our expectations, our loves, our perspectives are all turned upside down and inside out by the power of God's grace and love. This grace tries to draw us closer and closer to God and that, in turn, leads us deeper and deeper into a life of discipleship. That same grace surrounds each one of us whether we are aware of it or not, and it is that enfolding grace that unites us.

God came into the world primarily to give us grace, because after we had been created, we turned away and there was no way that we could get all the rules right. Through the gift of Christ upon the cross, grace becomes available to all of us if we receive it. That sounds like a great deal. God gives you life, you mess up, and God comes back in and says, "Okay, I'm not going to hold your sins against you anymore. I'm going to forgive you and give you a whole new life. I'm going to wipe the slate clean and I'm going to let you begin fresh and new." Now that sounds wonderful! You are given healing, newness of life, forgiveness, and a whole new horizon into which to live. You are given a new community of which to be a part.

There are other times when we get difficult things like what we read in the Scripture. What do we do with hard words like these? *Judge not, and you won't be judged.* It's a normal human tendency to judge when we see something we don't like. But Christ calls us into to a whole new way of being. When we respond to God's loving grace by repenting and committing ourselves, we become new creations: children of grace who are not only seen differently by God, but also see others differently.

Then come the words, "Condemn not." Judging you can do internally. Condemning is an externalization of that judgment. I want us to think about condemnation in the context of Christian community. Think for a moment about the diverse community gathered here today. All of us come from tremendously diverse backgrounds. We all have different ways that we experience God, different approaches to spirituality, and different gifts that we bring to the community of the Body of Christ. But we can allow these differences to become sources of conflict and division within the community. We often feel threatened by people who are different, who do things differently than we do, and so we are tempted to condemn and set ourselves apart: "Well, you don't do it the way I do it so you're really not the right kind of Christian." One person may get spiritual energy by serving the poor while another gets spiritual energy by praying for fifteen hours for someone. These are two totally different approaches and they are both fine. But, if someone who enjoys extended prayer condemns another by saying, "That person never prays," or if the person who ministers to the poor says, "You aren't doing enough by simply praying; you need to be involved in mission," then the Body of Christ begins to turn on itself. What happens when you do this? Don't condemn, and you won't be condemned. The church often gets so caught up in internal condemnation that we forget to see through the eyes of grace because we are judging one another. We are unable to become the kind of community that God has created us to be—a rich, diverse community that can show the world what it is like to love even when we are not alike. We are united by God's redemptive grace in spite of our diversity of opinion, of perspective, of experience: "Though we are many, we are one body."

The last piece of the Scripture is probably the toughest. "Forgive and you will be forgiven." Some understand this to mean that our forgiveness by God is contingent on our forgiveness of others; however, that sounds contrary to grace as unmerited forgiveness. What if we were to flip the statement and think about it in terms of community? What if forgiveness was not just about what God gives me and what I give another, but was really the environment we chose to create to enable our life together? That powerful thing that God came to give us, forgiveness, God calls us to share with one another. So this day we come together to the table to create community, to join together, to be blessed, healed, touched, cared for, strengthened, challenged, and oriented towards God.

As we prepare to come forward to break bread and share in the cup, symbols which remind us of God's act of love and forgiveness, consider those words:

Judge not. Condemn not. Forgive.

Consecration of the Elements

"Pour out your Holy Spirit on us gathered here, and on these gifts of bread and wine. Make them be for us the Body and Blood of Christ, that we may be for the world the Body of Christ, redeemed by his Blood.

By your Spirit make us one with Christ, one with each other, and one in ministry to all the world, until Christ comes in final victory and we feast at his heavenly banquet.

Through your Son Jesus Christ, with the Holy Spirit in your holy Church, all honor and glory is yours, almighty Father, now and for ever. Amen." (*The United Methodist Book of Worship*, p. 38)

(The pastor turns, takes the bread, and breaks it.)

Lord, continue to teach us this as we break this bread and share this cup so that we might be your community.

(The pastor turns, takes the cup and pitcher, and fills the cup. Communion servers are asked to come forward at this time.)

Holy Communion

"Peace to These Streets" by Graham Kendrick
©1996 Make Way Music (Admin. by Music Services)

(You may want to begin by playing this piece instrumentally and then move into congregational singing. It is very repetitive and can be used throughout the time of Holy Communion.)

The Invitation and Sending Forth

Service 6

The Body of Christ in Action

Scripture: Psalm 1

Entering the Story

We are called to be ones who are deeply rooted by the river of God's living water. In our "rootedness," we find strength in times of joy as well as in times of pain. As we grow, we bear fruit so that we might reach out to share the love and grace of Jesus Christ with the world so that others might also know God's touch.

Service Connections

This communion service involves the creation of relief bags for victims of natural disaster. It allows a hands-on mission opportunity for the entire congregation. Before the service, prepare an adequate number of stations in the worship space. Each station should contain boxes with all the items an individual will need to fill his or her bag. Have individuals or families pick up each item needed and return to their seats to assemble their bags. During the time in the service that the bags are created, it is very helpful to have the items and directions projected overhead. If the worship space does not have a projection system, an index card can be placed in each mission bag and referred to as needed.

The altar display should be very simple to allow for the mission bags to be placed on it during communion. If there are multiple services, a team can clear the table and restock mission items (if necessary) between services.

This particular service format does not include a separate Children's Time. Coordination with the children's ministry would allow for the children to participate in the mission project with their families. If children usually attend Children's Time in the service and move to a separate time of children's worship, explain that the children will be staying for the service. Also, if a congregational pattern exists in which parents attend worship while children attend Sunday School, plan for children to enter the worship service while the relief bags are being created. There are not always opportunities for multigenerational interaction in worship, but hands-on mission experiences facilitate that connection very well.

The following question might be asked: "Wouldn't it be easier to have a mission team assemble these bags at some other time than worship?" This would certainly be more efficient if you see the only outcome as the completion of the relief bags. But by allowing the entire congregation to participate in this activity, the congregation gains a new awareness of mission and outreach. A sense of unity in being the hands and feet of Christ in the world is experienced. The gathered body feels a sense of reaching beyond self and helping others. A service like this is a reminder that worship is not a compartmentalized activity but is connected to our lives and the life of the world beyond the confines of the hour.

A video clip demonstrating this service connection can be found on the DVD. Go to the "Video Clips" section, choose "Illustrative Clips," and select the video for "The Body of Christ in Action."

THE SERVICE

Welcome and Community Connection

Opening Music

"You Are My God" by Kent Henry
©1992 Integrity's Hosanna! Music (c/o Integrity Music, Inc.)

"Flow Like A River" by Billy Funk
©1997 Integrity's Hosanna! Music (c/o Integrity Music, Inc.)

"Spirit of the Living God" (UMH 393)

Consecration of the Elements

The elements are prepared at this time, though communion will be served at the close of the service. After the bread is broken, it is rewrapped in a towel taken from one of the mission boxes and placed next to the cup on the table.

The Pastoral Prayer and The Lord's Prayer

A Time of Explanation

Prior to the Scripture reading and sermon, it is important to prepare the congregation for their participation throughout the remainder of the service. Since including a mission project in the context of the service is seldom done on a regular basis, you will want to give a brief explanation that will help the congregation understand that they will be part of a sermon that will be finished sometime in the future.

Scripture Reading: Psalm 1

Encourage the congregation to think about this psalm as image-based communication, images that communicate the truth about what it means to be a human being and a child of God.

Pastoral Prayer of Preparation

Sermon Summary

The Psalms were originally songs and hymns that the ancient Hebrews used in worship to bring before God their joys, their sorrows, their fears, their hopes, and their praise. Though every psalm may not speak directly to your experience, you will encounter just about every fundamental human emotion and experience expressed in their words. Psalms of thanksgiving and praise express the joy and gratitude of the people for the faithfulness and love of God. Psalms of lament express feelings of being lost and alone, of being betrayed or separated from God. At times it is a more specific example, such as a person dealing with a betrayal of a friend. Sometimes there are words of deep emotion and often it is a simple expression of a person's realization of his or her place in the world, as can be found in Psalm 1.

This Psalm is simple and short—taking up less than a column—but what does it say? It says basically that we have a choice. We can live in the way that is according to God or we can live in the way that is not according to God. If you live in a way that is in accordance with God, you are like a tree planted by the water with roots that sink deep and yield fruit in its season. If you do not, you are like chaff that is swept away.

The Chattahoochee River is in Georgia, where I grew up. The course of the river changes and does not always benefit the trees that are planted nearby. The water flows and washes out all the dirt until the trees fall over. The image in the Psalm did not make sense to me until I visited Mount Rainier. Rising up from the center of a large plain is an ancient volcanic mountain covered with snow. Surrounding its base are primeval forests. Walking through the forest down into a valley, I was surrounded by huge trees. I felt ant-like under them. Streams of sunlight filtered through the branches, and birds were singing. I had never seen anything like it. It was amazing to imagine how long those trees had been there and how long that mountain had been there. From the perspective of a human being with a life span of seventy years, I saw myself as but a blip in time of God's ongoing creation! To see it all put me in my place and gave me a sense of perspective.

I kept walking and saw a place where the river split. Cold water flowed over smooth stones to the right and to the left. As the river split it went around an island of forest. The trees on the island in the fork of the river were three to four times larger than those I had just walked through. It seemed that an entire house could be carved out of a solid tree. Why, I wondered, were the trees on the island so much larger? They were fed and nourished by the water that ran deep around them and constantly gave them a source of life. Even when it did not rain and the rest of the forest had no water, the melting snow from Mount Rainier would flow into the river and nourish the roots of those trees. Even in times of drought or forest fire, that river served as a natural firebreak, protecting the trees from catastrophe. Because the trees were planted by the water, they were able to grow and stand even in the midst of difficulty.

Each of us, like those trees, is planted in the life of God. We are creations of God just like those trees—living beings. We can grow to become large "trees" in the forest of life, but what happens when the drought comes? What happens when the fire comes? We must be planted by the water and nourished by the ways and the words of God to endure the difficulties. If you are nourished by those ways and words, you will draw forth the life from that water and will bear fruit in due season.

There are many fruits that we bear as Christians. There is the "kneeling servant"- type fruit, the "giving"- type fruit, and the "words that we speak"- type fruit. I want to give you an opportunity today to bear fruit for someone who is not yet even aware that he or she is in trouble.

How many of you have ever lost electrical power? Though "roughing it" may start out as an adventure, it quickly becomes a pain. You have no control. What if a whole community had been destroyed by a series of tornados and nothing was left of the houses but the foundations? You would have nothing. Your church is destroyed. Everything is gone. What if this happened to us? What would we do?

Imagine yourself in this situation: You've been bused to another church or high school set up by the Red Cross. You have not brushed your teeth or eaten anything. You walk into a place, maybe like our church, and someone welcomes you and hands you a cup of coffee. They pray with you, hand you a sandwich, and find a place for you to sit and eat with your family. You are dirty, as there has been no place to bathe. You feel tired and "rootless." You have nothing left. Someone hands you a bag containing a towel, a toothbrush, soap, bandages, nail clippers, and a comb, and then points you toward a place where you can shower. They tell you a fresh set of clothes will be brought to you. They reassure you that you will have a place to sleep tonight. They leave you with the words "God loves you."

This is what will happen with the bags we assemble here today. Hundreds of these bags will be made and warehoused in an emergency center. Whether a tornado or hurricane, when disaster strikes, these relief bags will be ready. Do you know what this is? It's prevenient grace—grace that goes before need. It is a reminder that God loves us even before we have been broken or before we are aware we need help. Just like these relief bags sitting in a warehouse. Now you get to be part of prevenient grace this morning.

(Directions are now given for the relief bag project.)

A Time of Active Mission

This project may seem too time-consuming to do in a worship experience. However, with ushers in place to help guide and adequate stations prepared, this activity only takes a few minutes to accomplish. Strategically planned chaos works beautifully! People file in line, take their items, and move back to their seats to assemble their bags.

To allow for a few extra hands to help, involve your musicians with the usher team and let a CD play as people participate in the project. The following song is an excellent choice for this time:

"A Shadow in Your Light" by Lenny LeBlanc and Ava Aldridge
©1999 Integrity's Hosanna! Music/ASCAP & Len Songs Publishing (Admin. by Integrity's Hosanna! Music/ASCAP & Breneddie Music/ASCAP)

Holy Communion

It would have been easy to gather a group of ten volunteers to assemble these bags in a room. However, this is an opportunity for us to have an active and knowing part in the work that we as a congregation support. Now, hold your bag and close your eyes. Imagine having your house destroyed; imagine going three days without bathing (*pause*). Now open your eyes and see the bag again in a different light. Place your hands on the bag, and let's say a prayer:

God, we don't know when the activities of this sermon will be completed. We don't know when these bags will be opened. When they are, the items will come forth to wash a face that is dirty and tear stained. To clean fingers that have rummaged through mud to find wedding photos or that have carried a child through the night. We don't know, Lord, but you know. We know that you will be there to love. We ask that you would help these gifts that we offer, these fruits that come forth from our tree, to be instruments of your love. For we ask it in the name of Jesus Christ. Amen.

Communion servers are invited to come forward and the pastor takes bread, which was broken earlier in the service, from the towel and says:

Remember, someone at some point is going to open one of these bags, and in it, though there will not be bread, they will experience the body of Christ reaching out to touch them.

Music begins as people come forward for communion. The hymn, "Let Us Break Bread Together" (UMH 618), and "As Bread That is Broken" by Claire Cloniger and Paul Baloche [©1995 Integrity's Hosanna! Music (c/o Integrity Music, Inc.), Word Music, Inc. (a div. of Word Music Group, Inc.), Juniper Landing Music (Admin. by Word Music Group, Inc.)] provide an excellent combination for this service.

As people come forward, they take communion and place their mission bags on the altar. The altar then becomes a beautiful creation of "mission in motion" at the end of the service.

The Offering

As you listen to the words of this next song, be reminded that each and every moment you have the opportunity not only to draw from the life-giving water that God offers us, but also to be one who bears fruit in life for God in a tremendous number of ways.

"Life Means So Much" by Chris Rice
©2000 Clumsy Fly Music (Admin. by Word Music, Inc.)

The Invitation and Sending Forth

The pastor, standing in front of an altar table covered with mission packets wrapped in towels, holds one of the towels in his hands, looks at the congregation, and says:

What is this recurrent theme of towels? After supper Jesus got up and took off his outer clothes, put on a towel, and began to wash the disciples' feet. Could it be that God is transforming us into servants?

Invitation

Remember, no matter where you go, you are near to the river of God. Sink deep your roots. Go in peace and bear fruit. Amen.

For Future Thought

This service was created during a specific Volunteers In Mission project. Future uses of this service might revolve around specific mission needs within the global church family or the local community.

It is also important to note that pre-planning must be done in regard to the expense of the mission items for the service. The type of mission project chosen must be one that is financially feasible for the size of the congregation and budget with which you work. The initial idea of mission in motion can be modified in many ways and at many different times for future use.

Service 7

Through the Eyes of a Child

Scripture: Matthew 26:26–29

Entering the Story

Children see the world with a fresh and miraculous perspective. When they are allowed to experience the sacrament through story, the making of bread, and serving, they gain a deep and rich perspective of this activity. As they are encouraged to seek out the holy in the everyday, they develop a sense of active anticipation. In this service the congregation was allowed to experience communion through the eyes of a child.

Service Connections

The children's worship team prepared the bread for this service. A member of the congregation who loves to cook guided the children in mixing, kneading, and baking bread. While bread was baking, the senior pastor spent time sharing the story of communion with the children and teaching them "how" to serve communion to others. They practiced this act by taking turns serving each other. During the weekend, different children from the worship team served communion in all of the worship services. This would also be an excellent activity to do with a confirmation class.

A brief video clip demonstrating the children making bread can be found on the DVD. Go to the "Video Clips" section, choose "Illustrative Clips," and select the video for "Communion Through the Eyes of a Child."

THE SERVICE

Welcome and Community Connection

Opening Music

"Open the Eyes of My Heart" by Paul Baloche
©1997 Integrity's Hosanna! Music (c/o Integrity Music, Inc.)

"There Is None Like You" by Lenny LeBlanc
©1991 Integrity's Hosanna! Music (c/o Integrity Music, Inc.)

The Pastoral Prayer and The Lord's Prayer

The Offering

"What A Child is Meant to Be" by Kathryn Scott
© 2000 Vineyard Songs (UK/EIRE), Admin. by Music Services

Scripture Reading: Matthew 26:26–29

Pastoral Prayer of Preparation

Sermon Summary

A few weeks ago the members of our children's worship team were sent out to be "God reporters." We gave them disposable cameras and asked them to take pictures where they saw examples of God's love, God's people serving, God's people giving, God's creative activity, and God's beauty in creation. So they went out looking for God, focused on discerning where and how God is active in the world. They began to "see" the answer to their questions because they were actively anticipating. They were developing what I like to call "Advent eyes," eyes that actively anticipate the coming of God. We are hoping to build this receptivity into their hearts and minds.

We gathered a few nights ago in the kitchen and made bread with the children. They mixed flour, milk, and other ingredients in the food processor and made a huge wad of dough. They put it on the counter and kneaded the dough. We added yeast, but it became unleavened because I think they pounded on it so hard the yeast died, or at least gave up. The bread was a little flat, but *they* made it.

Covered with flour, we sat down to remember the stories of bread in the Bible as our loaves baked. We talked about how the Israelites, enslaved in Egypt, cried out to God, and God sent Moses to lead them to freedom. When it came time for them to leave, they didn't even have time to put yeast in the bread before they left, so it was unleavened.

We talked about how the Hebrew people wandered in the desert. They didn't have any food or a snack truck following them around. There wasn't much to eat in the desert but God provided bread—manna from heaven.

We talked about the time when Jesus gathered with the disciples around a table and celebrated that Passover with unleavened bread, remembering how God had freed their ancestors from bondage and sustained them. Jesus took that moment and incorporated all of history and their entire story and said, "It is no longer just about that, but this is my body, broken for you, and my blood which is poured out for you. Every time you eat this bread and drink this cup, remember me."

After the stories, we went into the worship area and practiced serving communion. We practiced breaking the bread, holding it, looking into people's eyes and saying, "This is the body of Christ given for you." We held the cup and said, "This is the blood of Christ for you." These are our children and now their eyes have been changed. They will never be able to see a piece of bread the same way. They will never be able to go into a church and experience a service the same way. Now they see with Advent eyes. My hope is that all of us will see with Advent eyes—actively watching and listening for the presence of God.

Consecration of the Elements

This probably looks similar to the bread that Jesus used. *(The pastor holds up a loaf of bread that the children made.)* Jesus took the bread and he thanked God for it and *(breaking)* he broke it. He said, "This is my body which is broken for you." *(The pastor picks up the pitcher and pours the juice into the cup.)* And he took the cup, gave thanks, and said, "This is the cup of the new covenant. This is the blood that is shed for you for the forgiveness of sins. Every time you eat the bread and you drink the cup remember me until I come again. "

(Communion servers are invited to come forward at this time.)

Lord, pour out your Spirit upon each one of us gathered here today. Touch our heart and minds. Help us to see where it is that we are far from you. Perhaps we need to be freed from seeing and expecting only negative things. We ask, God, that you would give us Advent eyes—eyes that watch for your coming, your blessing, your peace, your hope, and your joy. Bless this bread and this juice that they might be for us your body and your blood, that they might nourished us so we can become your body in this world. Forgive us, Lord, and free us that we might be joyfully obedient. In Jesus' name we pray. Amen.

Holy Communion

"Eagle's Wings" by Reuben Morgan
©1998 Reuben Morgan (Hillsong), Admin. in U.S. & Canada by Integrity's Hosanna! Music

"On Eagle's Wings" (UMH 143)

The Invitation and Sending Forth

Service
8

Can We Drink This Cup?

Scripture: Luke 22:42

Entering the Story

Participating in the sacrament of communion is an activity of community. In the act of sharing the cup of life, we open ourselves to a deeper bond of relationship as brothers and sisters in Christ. Our sharing can be an invitation to be real, present, and open to one another in joy, sadness, and all of life.

Service Connection

A clear glass pitcher and large, clear, globed glass chalices were used for this service. These items can be easily and inexpensively acquired, and makes for a very nice visual effect.

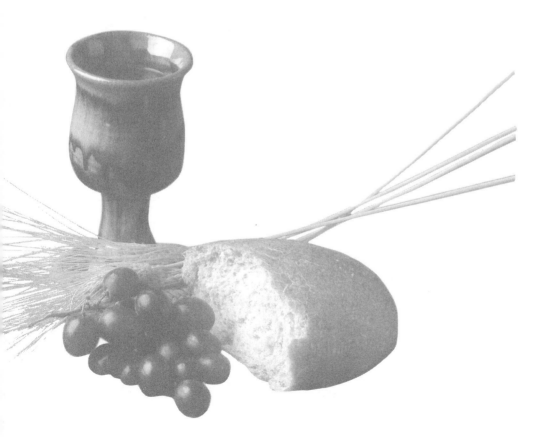

THE SERVICE

Welcome and Community Connection

Children's Time Suggestion

A possible suggestion for this children's time would be to focus on the cup as the "Cup of Life."

Have you ever felt very happy and very full of God? That feels good doesn't it? There are other times when we feel sad or lonely. Then it feels like our "cup" is closer to empty. One of the things about being able to come together in church is that we can share our lives with each other whether we are happy or sad; whether things are going well or life seems difficult. When we gather together as a church we share life with each other. We hold each other up, we share each other's lives, and we share in the one faith that holds us together.

The children share in Communion with the pastor.

Opening Music

"Holy, Holy, Holy" (UMH 64)

"Holy" by Brenton Brown
©2001 Vineyard Songs (UK/Eire), Admin. by Music Services

The Pastoral Prayer and The Lord's Prayer

The Offering

"Fill My Cup, Lord" (UMH 641)

Scripture Reading: Luke 22:42

Pastoral Prayer of Preparation

Sermon Summary

This particular sermon is based upon the book Can You Drink the Cup? *by Henri Nouwen. In this book, Nouwen recounts the story of sharing communion with his friends in a facility for the mentally challenged, and his meditation on what it means to **hold** the cup, **lift** the cup, and **drink** from the cup. He realized that when those gathered there did this themselves, the act of communion become real to them. Nouwen pondered the question if the cup is a symbol for our lives, then what would it mean for each of us to really take hold of our life, not just to see it there but to hold it, and accept the life that God has given us in all of its completeness?*

60

Several stories are used to illustrate how we often miss holding the cup because we are busy and distracted. We often miss lifting the cup because we try to do it on our own instead of relying on the help of the gathered body. We must be present to others, to lift the life that is ours in community. It is not always easy to say, "This is me, and I share it with you, because I believe you value who I am, and I value you . . . I celebrate with you," or "See how my cup is cracked?"

In closing, the theme of drinking the cup is reflected upon as choosing to live life fully in times of joy as well as in times of difficulty.

Imagine drinking something. What was the best drink you ever had? Was it something that had a little umbrella in it, or a big latte, piled high with whipped cream and chocolate sprinkles? How about a very cold cup of water on a very hot day? You can remember those good things. It is easy to drink those, to celebrate those pleasures, to appreciate beautiful things. But drinking is not always a pleasant memory . . .

I remember one of the most difficult drinks I have ever had. It happened when I went to visit a woman who had become immobile and isolated. I found out that this woman had become confined to her trailer, so I went to visit her. When I opened the door, silverfish and roaches dripped from the bottom of the door frame. The floor crunched as I walked. She sat in a dark room with the TV blaring cartoons. The curtain moved with bugs. Now, I don't know if she was testing me, or genuinely concerned for my thirstiness, but she offered me a glass of water. "The glasses are on the kitchen counter, "she said. The kitchen counter was in plain view from where she sat in her chair. I looked at those clouded glasses thinking to myself, "Hot water . . . Lysol," but what would it have said to her if I were not willing to share a glass of water in her house? And so that afternoon I had a little "roach-foot tea." Luckily, I didn't die. More importantly, by not refusing this woman's simple hospitality, I didn't risk rejecting her. There are times when holding, lifting, and drinking from the cup is difficult. As brothers and sisters in Christ we are given the privilege of sharing the cups of our lives together.

Consecration of the Elements

The pastor turns to pick up the cup and pitcher from the table. Then, facing the congregation in silence, he fills the cup and breaks the bread.

When you come to this table I want you to think about the life that God has given you—life that is so easily missed at times. Ask yourself are you willing to hold it? To take it and to hold it? To become truly aware of the life you live? Not to hide it, but to see those to whom God has drawn you in community and family? Are we willing to celebrate this life together, or help each other with our brokenness? As we share, as individuals and as a community, we become able to drink fully the cup that is life.

(Communion servers are invited to come forward.)

This is the Blood of the new covenant. This is the Body of Christ. Lord, pour out your Spirit upon all who gather here and upon these gifts of bread and of wine. Help them be for us so much more than symbols; help them be for us a path into life abundant and eternal. Lord, where we are broken, where we are far from you, where we are sinful, we ask that you would forgive us and wash us clean. Help us to see the life that you give us that we might live it more fully. Redeemed by your blood, we ask this in the name of Jesus. Amen.

Holy Communion

During this time a soloist or vocal ensemble sings "Can We Drink This Cup?" (music score included on the DVD).

The Invitation and Sending Forth

Invitation

Now, each of you, filled with the Spirit of Christ, carry forth that light into the world and share it. Go in peace. Amen.

Service 9

Walking Today Where Jesus Walked

Scripture: Matthew 21:1–11; Luke 22:7–71; Luke 23: 32–46

Entering the Story

God knows us and loves us no matter who we are or what we have been through. We are called to enter into the story and accept God's grace. We are called to receive God's salvation and in turn offer it to the world.

Service Connections

We often pass right over the death of Christ during Holy Week. We come to church for Palm Sunday and Easter Sunday, skipping from Jesus' triumphal entry to his triumphant resurrection, and miss participating in the Maundy Thursday service. This service is constructed to help the congregation experience more fully the events of Holy Week. Though it could be considered a drama in its entirety, it allows for congregational participation, including the elements one would find in a "normal" service.

The children's worship team helped prepare the altar and setting for the Palm Sunday service using a large drop cloth from the hardware store and washable paint. In the parking lot, we gathered with the children and talked about the last week in Jesus' life. We talked about what was it like to have been alive during the time Jesus was here on earth; to have walked where Jesus walked. After a time of discussion, the children took off their shoes, and we painted their feet with brown paint. As they continued to think about walking where Jesus walked, they began to walk across the canvas spread out in the parking lot. From one side to the other they walked, with frequent "re-paintings" of their feet.

After this was completed the altar design team went to work. They took the canvas and made it the floor of the table area, which was now the main area where the drama would occur during the service. This area was used as a place of home and gathering at the beginning of the service, but later became the scene of the crucifixion at the end of the service. At the center was a table that remained throughout the service. As you will see in the clip from this service, it is a simple set allowing for much flexibility.

To view a brief clip from this drama, go to the "Video Clips" section, choose "Illustrative Clips," and select the video for "Walking Today Where Jesus Walked."

THE SERVICE

Welcome and Explanation of Service

It is important to allow for a time of brief explanation of this worship service. Setting the stage for what will happen allows the congregation to be open to experiencing God in a different way from that to which they are accustomed.

SCENE I

(This scene begins with all lights at 100%.)

Band: "Sing Praises"(as found on Third Day's album, *Come Together*)

The band, stage left, plays introduction until the singing begins.

As the song begins, the children enter from the back of the worship area waving their palms and make their way to center stage. The typical group of children involved in singing and participating in the processional music for Palm Sunday are those who participate in children's choir and Sunday school programming. Also included in the group are those children who will be cast throughout the rest of the service. They are dressed in biblical costumes, while the rest of the children are in normal clothing. Make this an intentional point of inclusivity for the children in the service by inviting all children to participate even if they were not involved in the rehearsals.

Have the Vocal Ensemble dress in black pants and shirts with colorful overshirts or jackets that will be removed later to change the tone from parade to passion. They are located stage left with the band and are standing and ready for their part in the Scripture reading.

Have two youth readers in costume (part of the acting cast) read the Scripture from the space designated for Scripture reading throughout the service.

The lights are at 100% stage left, center stage, and house.

Scripture: Matthew 21:1–11

Youth 1: "As they approached Jerusalem and came to Bethphage on the Mount of Olives, Jesus sent two disciples, saying to them, 'Go to the village ahead of you, and at once you will find a donkey tied there, with her colt by her. Untie them and bring them to me. If anyone says anything to you, tell him that the Lord needs them, and he will send them right away.'"

Youth 2: "This took place to fulfill what was spoken through the prophet:

> Say to the Daughter of Zion,
> 'See, your king comes to you,
> gentle and riding on a donkey,
> on a colt, the foal of a donkey.'"

Youth 1: "The disciples went and did as Jesus had instructed them. They brought the donkey and the colt, placed their cloaks on them, and Jesus sat on them. A very large crowd spread their cloaks on the road, while others cut branches from the trees and spread them on the road. The crowds that went ahead of him and those that followed shouted:

Vocal Ensemble: *'Hosanna to the Son of David!*
Blessed is he who comes in the name of the Lord!
Hosanna in the highest!'"

Youth 2: "When Jesus entered Jerusalem, the whole city was stirred and asked, 'Who is this?' The crowds answered,

Vocal Ensemble: *'This is Jesus, the prophet from Nazareth in Galilee.'"*

The children and the Vocal Ensemble now begin singing the song, "Sing Praises." As it is finished, the band continues to play while all of the children who aren't in the cast exit stage left. Those in the cast stay center stage. The lights in the room gradually fade out as the last of the children leave the room.

As the lights go out, the Vocal Ensemble is seated. They quietly remove their colorful jackets and put them under their chairs. The Youth in Scene II and the Narrator take their places.

SCENE II

Lights 100% stage right; house lights off. The Narrator should be a fifth- or sixth-grade boy or girl. Memorization of the narration is not absolutely necessary, but preferred.

Narrator: Can you imagine? Can you imagine being in Jerusalem that day? I think it must have been amazing!

I'm just your average, ordinary kid. I go to school, to church. I like to play with friends and I love _____ and hate _____. I love life and I love living in the technological world we have today. I don't remember life before the Internet! But sometimes, when I hear all these Bible stories about Jesus, I wonder what it was like to really *be* there while Jesus was here on earth.

Think about that day of the parade! Parades are so exciting. People even arrive early and camp out hours before the parade begins just to get a good spot. But can you imagine being alongside the road when the Lord of the Universe rode by? Wow! I think it would have been amazing to be in the crowd that day. I wonder what it must have been like to walk where Jesus walked?

(Lights fade out stage right on narrator and come up 75% on the Vocal Ensemble standing stage left.)

Vocal Ensemble: Sings first verse of "I Walked Today Where Jesus Walked" by G. Ohara (© G. Shirmer, Inc.)

(After the song, lights fade out on Vocal Ensemble—now seated—and come up on center stage 100%.)

SCENE III

*(**Youth 3** should be a girl and **Youth 6** should be a boy.)*

Youth 3: Did you go to the parade?

Youth 1: Yeah, it was cool!

Youth 4: Did you go?

Youth 5: No, I had too much homework. I have a big scroll due tomorrow.

Child 1: We went even though my Mom said it was "much ado about nothing."

Youth 1: Nothing? I think Jesus is a little more than nothing. Did you see him heal that blind man the other day?

Youth 3: And he raised Lazarus from the dead!

Child 2: And he healed the crippled woman!

Child 3: Not to mention those ten lepers he healed on his way to Jerusalem!

Child 1: Who knows if all that really happened? Were you there?

Child 5: Well, I was there when he fed all those people! I gave him my fish and bread. Trust me, my mom didn't pack my lunch for 5,000 that day. He took my five loaves and two fish and fed everybody there!

Youth 5: Well, I've heard people say he hangs out with the wrong crowd.

Child 6: (*youngest child on the set, tugging on the sleeve of the older sibling*) Isn't Jesus the man who had dinner with the tax collector the other day?

Youth 1: He's the one!

Child 6: My dad called the tax collector a…

Youth 1: Let's just say he said the tax collector is a man he wouldn't want to have dinner with.

Youth 6: (*comes running in excitedly from stage left*) Hey, guess what?! Jesus just threw the money changers out of the temple. It was great! Stirred up quite a commotion.

Child 1: Were you there?

Youth 6: Well, I wasn't supposed to be, but I snuck in the side door of the temple for a better view.

Youth 3: Was he angry?

Youth 6: I would say he was a little miffed! He said, "My house will be a house of prayer, but you have made it 'a den of robbers.'"

Mother 1: (*enters from stage left with a large basket of bread*) Speaking of a house of prayer–(*directing these statements to three individual children*) I'm praying all of you are going to be washed up for supper when your father, and your father, and your father, get home. All of you are eating here tonight, so scoot. Everyone finish your chores, your Hebrew homework, and get washed up. Tell your mothers they can come over when they are ready.

Everyone exits stage right and moves to the back of the worship area except Mother 1, Youth 3, and a few small children who will participate in singing the next song as supper is prepared. Mother 1 and Youth 3 are preparing the bread during this scene while the small children gather close by.

Mother 1: (*To youth 3 calling her by name*) _____, dear, get the fire ready. Your father will be here any moment.

Youth 3: Yes, Mother. Mother, what do you think about Jesus?

Mother 1: Well, I think he makes a lot of sense.

Youth 3: You don't think he hangs out with the wrong crowd?

Mother 1: (*reflecting*) I think maybe he "hangs out," as you put it, with whomever he comes in contact. He doesn't seem to segregate people into the categories our society has established. He spends time with everyone—everyone who really needs to hear the words he is speaking. I think we probably *all* need to hear the words he speaks.

Youth 3: Why do you think so many people are angry about his teaching, especially the church leaders?

Mother 1: Well, _____, people don't like change. Jesus' way of thinking requires some change of thought. For instance, Jesus went to Zacchaeus' house the other day, and you would have thought the world was ending. Nobody stopped to think about what it did for Zacchaeus. No one has been nice to that man in years. Jesus made a connection with him that was life-changing.

Men enter from stage left with a huge catch of fish. Real fish were discussed for this service, but the table/altar design team found fish "props" that looked so real they were used so that the odor of fish did not become part of the service!

Father 1: It was a good day's catch! Is everyone ready to eat?

Small Children on the Set: (*joyful*) Yes!!

Older Male Youth: I've been ready to eat since we left the boat!

Father 2: What a day! A celebration feast we will have this evening. More fish than we can say grace over!

Mother 1: I sent the children off to wash up. Why don't you all do the same. We will finish up here.

The men grumble and exit stage left as the lights fade out on center stage. Mother 1, Youth 3, and small children stay in place for the song and lights come up 100% stage right on the narrator.

Narrator: When Jesus walked here on earth, he spent time with the people. He didn't segregate himself. Jesus didn't build walls; he built relationships. He taught love for all people—even our enemies. His teaching allowed for *all* people to have a sense of hope, a sense of joy.

(Lights out stage right on the narrator and lights come up 100% center stage.)

Mother 1, Youth 3, and Small Children: *Sing "Blessed Are You" by Howard Hanger (available from www.howardhanger.com). The first verse and chorus are done as a solo by Youth 3; other voices enter the second time through the song.*

After the song is finished, lights fade out on center stage and come up 100% stage right on the narrator. The entire cast moves to center stage in the darkness as the narrator begins. Baskets filled with chicken tenders are brought to the dinner scene to go along with the bread.

Narrator: Jesus not only focused on the importance of building relationships and community with each other, but with God as well. He taught that time spent talking to God should not be concerned with eloquent speech or displaying a large vocabulary. He encouraged simplicity. Jesus gave us a model of prayer that we still use today. A prayer that says, "God, you are awesome." A prayer that asks that God's kingdom be alive and well not only in heaven, but right here on earth—today. A prayer that asks for God's provision for us, God's forgiveness of us, God's deliverance for us, and God's guidance for us. A prayer that reminds us that we not only ask God for these things, but that we in turn participate as "God reflectors," sharing grace, forgiveness, love, and acceptance with others. Jesus modeled for us a God that listens, a God that desires a relationship with all God's children. Will you take a moment with me this morning to talk to God?

The Narrator leads the congregation in the Lord's Prayer. As the last line of the prayer is reached, the lights go out stage right on the narrator and come up 100% on the entire cast seated center stage, all finishing the Lord's Prayer with the congregation. After a hearty group "Amen" is said, they begin to pass baskets filled with bread and chicken. This is a great "bonus" for the children in the service as they are actually having a snack while the adult conversation happens in the scene.

SCENE IV

(A candle is lit on the table by one of the adults as the scene begins.)

Mother 2: Things were certainly stirred up today after Jesus threw the money changers out of the temple.

Mother 3: Well, he should have thrown them out. The street merchants shouldn't be set up in the temple!

Mother 2: I agree, but I think he's beginning to really heat up the officials. I'm afraid they are going to throw him in jail—or worse!

Mother 1: But he hasn't done anything wrong. How can they throw him in jail?

Father 1: Speaking out the way he has is going to count as "wrong enough" when it comes to what they *can* and *cannot* do with him.

Father 2: When they ask him questions, his answers only anger them. It's rather funny actually. He always has an answer that throws them off. You can sense their anger at his reply.

Father 1: Yeah, like the other day with the tax questions. He sure nailed 'em.

Father 3: And with such simplicity. I would never have thought to just take a coin and look at whose picture is on it!

Father 1: "Give to Caesar what is Caesar's and to God what is God's." He didn't leave them much room for a comeback.

Lights fade out center stage and come up 100% on the narrator stage right. The baskets that held the bread are emptied by the cast into a large basket on the set that has a trash bag hidden in it. The baskets now are ready for the offering when the time comes. They wait patiently in darkness.

Narrator: Jesus' response in tough situations seemed to find roots in simplicity. But the depth of his simplicity was amazing. His response on taxation was right to the point; but what depth of wisdom it displayed.

We pay taxes today, but none of us pay them very joyfully though they are an integral part of our economic system. Even I know that when I save up for a new video game, I also have to save enough for the taxes. I also know that I need to give back to God a portion of what God has given me. What's the difference? Giving to God is something I can have a joyful attitude about! Why? Because God only wants only a small portion back of what I have received.

When we give back to God, we are really celebrating the abundance of what God has provided us. We are not just paying a fee for something. Just as they had the opportunity to give back to God long ago, we still have the opportunity to do the same today.

Vocal Ensemble: "I Give My All" by Kristen McCallum
©1999 Kristen McCallum/Poetking Publishing (Admin. by Poetking Publishing)

This song was chosen because it fit the theme and because it is a congregational hymn. This is a time for the congregation to sing, so choosing a hymn or song that would be known by your individual congregation here would be important.

The lights in the worship area come up 100%, including the house lights, with the vocal ensemble standing. The cast, paired one adult and one child, become the ushers. They move from the front toward the back passing the offering plates, with another person right behind them with the attendance registers. The size of the cast should provide a few extra people walking from front to back if any assistance with the children is necessary. Once the offering baskets move through the congregation, the house lights begin to fade out. The lights remain on the vocal ensemble until the song is finished.

Lights fade out on the Vocal Ensemble stage left and come up 100% stage right on the narrator. The four cast members, two youth and two adults, who will serve as readers in the next scene make their way to the microphones.

Narrator: Jesus could have taken a completely different approach to his time here on earth. He could have stayed in the temple every day, reading Scripture and conversing with those who already knew the right answers. He could have spent all his time discussing repentance, forgiveness, love, acceptance, and new life behind closed doors with the religious leaders of the day. Instead, he took an approach to ministry that some people had a hard time understanding. Like all those miracles he performed—they weren't necessarily *required* to fulfill his task here on earth. Those miracles were yet another example of Jesus' genuine love and care for those around him.

Even those closest to him, his disciples, didn't always understand his human relations policy. At times they struggled to understand his teachings. They, too, heard what others were saying and often worried about those with whom he associated. Jesus reminded those who criticized his ways that he was sent for the lost: "It is not the healthy who need a doctor, but the sick. For I have not come to call the righteous, but sinners" (Luke 5:30b–32). There were even times when the disciples wanted to send people away, and Jesus would have to remind them that they were to have "open hearts, open minds, and open doors."

Jesus loved his disciples and spent time teaching them and preparing them so that eventually they would "go and make disciples of all nations, baptizing them in the name of the Father and of the Son and of the Holy Spirit, and teaching them to obey everything He had commanded them—for He would be with them always." But they did not fully understand the events that were yet to come. Their leader would soon be hung on a cross, and they would have more questions than answers.

Lights fade out on the narrator stage right and come up 100% on center stage as twelve members of the cast, including representation of both male and female, children, youth and adults, walk from the back of the room down the aisles to center stage. When they reach the front, they form a straight line and kneel at the table.

SCENE V

(Lights are at 75% on the readers.)

Scripture: Luke 22:7–71 (NIV)

Reader 1: "Then came the day of Unleavened Bread on which the Passover lamb had to be sacrificed. Jesus sent Peter and John, saying, 'Go and make preparations for us to eat the Passover.' 'Where do you want us to prepare for it?' they asked. He replied,

Reader 2: 'As you enter the city, a man carrying a jar of water will meet you. Follow him to the house that he enters, and say to the owner of the house, 'The Teacher asks: Where is the guest room, where I may eat the Passover with my disciples?' He will show you a large upper room, all furnished. Make preparations there."

Reader 3: They left and found things just as Jesus had told them. So they prepared the Passover.

(Pastor moves into the set center stage to take the bread and cup.)

Reader 4: When the hour came, Jesus and his apostles reclined at the table. And he said to them,

(A soft instrumental introduction to the upcoming song can begin at this point.)

Reader 2: "I have eagerly desired to eat this Passover with you before I suffer. For I tell you, I will not eat it again until it finds fulfillment in the kingdom of God."

Reader 3: After taking the cup, he gave thanks and said,

Reader 2: "Take this and divide it among you. For I tell you I will not drink again of the fruit of the vine until the kingdom of God comes."

Reader 3: And he took bread, gave thanks and broke it, and gave it to them, saying,

Reader 2: "This is my Body given for you; do this in remembrance of me."

(Pastor breaks the bread.)

Reader 3: In the same way, after the supper he took the cup, saying,

Reader 2: "This cup is the new covenant in my Blood, which is poured out for you."

(Pastor pours juice in cup.)

Vocal Ensemble Response: *"Remember Me" (score included on the DVD) is sung while the twelve cast members receive communion.*

(Lights to 50% on the Vocal Ensemble stage left.)

After the twelve cast members are served by the pastors, they are then given chalices and bread, and turn to serve the congregation. The house lights are brought up to 75%, and the congregation comes forward to participate in the sacrament of Holy Communion. Instrumental music continues while the congregation is served and as this time comes to a close the Vocal Ensemble and the congregation sing the words to "Remember Me" several more times.

As everyone is seated, all house lights fade out and lights come up 100% on the narrator, stage left. The twelve members of the cast make their way up the aisles to the back of the room where the rest of the cast is gathered.

Narrator: (*more intense*) In the midst of that meal with his disciples, things began to get a little weird. Jesus told the disciples that one of them would betray him; that one of them would deny him. It was about to be "uncool" to be a follower of Jesus and he knew his time on earth was drawing to a close. I'm not sure I would have been brave enough to walk where Jesus walked at this point in his life.

(Lights fade out stage right on the narrator and come up 75% on the readers.)

Reader 4: Jesus went out as usual to the Mount of Olives, and his disciples followed him. On reaching the place, he said to them,

Reader 2: "Pray that you will not fall into temptation."

Reader 4: He withdrew about a stone's throw beyond them, knelt down and prayed,

Reader 2: "Father, if you are willing, take this cup from me; yet not my will, but yours be done." An angel from heaven appeared to him and strengthened him.

Reader 4: And being in anguish, he prayed more earnestly, and his sweat was like drops of blood falling to the ground.

Reader 1: When he rose from prayer and went back to the disciples, he found them asleep, exhausted from sorrow.

Reader 2: "Why are you sleeping?" he asked them. "Get up and pray so that you will not fall into temptation."

Reader 1: While he was still speaking a crowd came up, and the man who was called Judas, one of the Twelve, was leading them. He approached Jesus to kiss him, but Jesus asked him,

Reader 2: "Judas, are you betraying the Son of Man with a kiss?"

Reader 1: When Jesus' followers saw what was going to happen, they said, "Lord, should we strike with our swords?" And one of them struck the servant of the high priest, cutting off his right ear. But Jesus answered,

Reader 2: "No more of this!"

Reader 1: And he touched the man's ear and healed him.

Vocal Ensemble and Soloist: "The Only Way" by Cindy Morgan
©1998 Word Music, Inc. (a div. of Word Music Group, Inc.)

The lights go out on the readers and come up 100% center stage and 100% stage left on the Vocal Ensemble, standing, and soloist. The dancer enters from the darkness and moves into the light center stage. Three men from the Vocal Ensemble move to the back of the room and toward the end of the song move down the aisles to carry the dancer off in the middle of the song. This is easier to comprehend visually and can be seen on the DVD clip section.

As the song ends, the lights center stage and stage right fade out and light comes up 75% on the readers.

SCENE VI

*During this reading, the older male youth from the cast slowly drags a very large cross to the center of the set. A red spotlight follows him. A holder for the cross is built into the center of the set, and he places the cross in it once he reaches the center. Once it is placed in the holder, the older male youth kneels at the foot of the cross. The red spotlight remains on the cross, shadowing the youth kneeling. The rest of the cast follows him to center stage and kneels, filling the set. Quiet instrumental music is played underneath the reading as this is taking place. Either play a recap of something used earlier, or another hymn such as "Were You There" (**UMH** 288). Lights come up to 50% on the readers as they begin.*

SCRIPTURE: Matthew 27:27–37 (NIV)

Reader 3: Then the governor's soldiers took Jesus into the Praetorium and gathered the whole company of soldiers around him. They stripped him and put a scarlet robe on him, and then twisted together a crown of thorns and set it on his head. They put a staff in his right hand and knelt in front of him and mocked him. "Hail, king of the Jews!" they said. They spit on him, and took the staff and struck him on the head again and again. After they had mocked him, they took off the robe and put his own clothes on him. Then they led him away to crucify him.

Reader 4: As they were going out, they met a man from Cyrene, named Simon, and they forced him to carry the cross. They came to a place called Golgotha (which means The Place of the Skull). There they offered Jesus wine to drink, mixed with gall; but after tasting it, he refused to drink it. When they had crucified him, they divided up his clothes by casting lots. And sitting down, they kept watch over him there.

Scripture: Luke 23:32–46 (NIV)

Two other men, both criminals, were also led out with him to be executed. When they came to the place called the Skull, there they crucified him, along with the criminals—one on his right, the other on his left. Jesus said,

Reader 2: "Father, forgive them, for they do not know what they are doing."

Reader 4: And they divided up his clothes by casting lots.

Reader 1: The people stood watching, and the rulers even sneered at him. They said, "He saved others; let him save himself if he is the Christ of God, the Chosen One."

The soldiers also came up and mocked him. They offered him wine vinegar and said, "If you are the king of the Jews, save yourself."

There was a written notice above him, which read: THIS IS THE KING OF THE JEWS.

One of the criminals who hung there hurled insults at him: "Aren't you the Christ? Save yourself and us!"

But the other criminal rebuked him. "Don't you fear God," he said, "since you are under the same sentence? We are punished justly, for we are getting what our deeds deserve. But this man has done nothing wrong."

Then he said, "Jesus, remember me when you come into your kingdom."

Jesus answered him,

Reader 2: "I tell you the truth, today you will be with me in paradise."

Reader 3: It was now about the sixth hour, and darkness came over the whole land until the ninth hour, for the sun stopped shining. And the curtain of the temple was torn in two. Jesus called out with a loud voice,

Reader 2: "Father, into your hands I commit my spirit."

One of the cast members turns and blows the light on the table out. The Vocal Ensemble collectively inhales loudly, causing a great "gasp."

When he had said this, he breathed his last.

The Vocal Ensemble's gasp is released on cue. The lights fade out on the readers, and they move to kneel center stage with the rest of the cast. The red light remains glowing center stage, and the lights are brought up 50% on the vocal ensemble.

Vocal Ensemble: "When Jesus Wept" (*The Faith We Sing* 2106)

The lights fade out on the Vocal Ensemble stage left. The narrator walks into the red light, in the midst of the cast, and an additional 25% of regular lighting is added for lighting support. Cast members carefully turn from a kneeling position to a seated position focused on the narrator.

Narrator: It would have been so sad to walk through those last hours—to see how Jesus was treated, to have been helpless in stopping them from hurting him. I just can't imagine. If I could go back there now, I would want to say to all the disciples, to all those who were sad *(addressed to cast)*, "Wait! It's not over. This fulfills the prophecy of the Scriptures. Jesus told you 'We will go to Jerusalem, and everything that is written by the prophets about the son of Man will be fulfilled. He will be handed over to the Gentiles. They will mock him, insult him, spit on him, flog him, and kill him." But don't you remember the last part of what he said? "On the third day he will rise again."

(Narrator turns to face the congregation.) I can't go back and say that to the disciples in their moment of grief, but I can say it where I walk today. This is not the end of the story; there is more! The death of Christ is an essential part of the Easter story, but it is not the end of the story. The cross leads to an empty tomb; death leads to resurrection, to new life. God's gift of his only Son keeps on giving each and every day. Just as Jesus shared his message beyond societal walls, to all people while he was here on earth, the message is to be shared the same way today. God knows you and loves you no matter who you are or what you have been through. We are called to be ones who accept and pour out God's grace, ones who receive God's salvation and in turn offer it to the world.

(The attention of the narrator and cast focuses stage left to the soloists and choir.)

Vocal Ensemble and Soloists:

"There Is Always One More Time" as found on Harry Connick, Jr.'s album, 30. *(K. Hirsh-D. Pomus EMI Blackwood Music, Inc. obo itself and Morning Mist Music (BMI)/Stazybo Music)*

A Time of Reflection, Invitation, and Sending Forth

At the close of this song the pastor moves to center stage as house lights and stage lighting is brought to 100%. The pastor takes a moment to reflect and offer an invitation and sending forth. As people leave, a recap of "There Is Always One More Time" is played and sung.

If you have multiple services, this is the time when several people should be ready to re-supply the set with needed items: fresh bread, fresh napkins in the baskets, a new candle, fresh chicken prepared, trash removed, etc. This service lasts approximately one hour.

Service 10

World Communion

Scripture: Matthew 5:13

Entering the Story

Across the face of the earth, in different communities and different cultures, Christians gather to celebrate the sacrament. This service was designed to help people experience themselves as part of this global phenomenon. The hope was that they would both experience the vastness and extent of God's love as well as the personal touch of God's healing grace in their own lives.

THE SERVICE

Welcome and Community Connection

Children's Time Suggestion

(Gather pictures of Christ from various cultures.)

No one really knows what Jesus looked like while he was on earth. However, people from all over the world love him, learn from him, and worship him. Sometimes when we look at people from different cultures or countries, we see our differences, but when we come together to share Communion we remember that even though we are many different types of people we are one in Jesus.

Opening Music

"O For a Thousand Tongues to Sing" (UMH 57)

"How Good and Pleasant" by Tommy Walker
©2000 Integrity's Praise! Music (c/o Integrity Music, Inc.)

Scripture Reading: Matthew 5:13

The Pastoral Prayer and the Lord's Prayer

Think for a moment of five things with which you are currently struggling. These may be large or small things, personal or financial things. Now think of five things you are struggling with in people you know, in people you love, and in people you care for. Now, think about five things that make you extremely happy to be alive, things that are a joy for you.

You just thought of things that probably no one else thought of in exactly the same way. Connected to the whole history of your life, these things are a big part of who you are. Sometimes these things seem private, more than you can handle or more than you can understand on your own. However, God, the one who created all there is, knows all things, even the ones you are afraid to bring to mind. God knows things that you are not even aware of that cause you pain. Right now, God wants to reach out and touch you, bringing you comfort, peace, direction, strength, and fulfillment in joy, purpose, hope, renewal—whatever it is that you might need at this moment. Rather than praying aloud I want you, you creatures of God, to simply be in God's presence and lift those things you have thought of to God. Picture God like this: put those things in God's hands, or climb up in those hands and let God hold you. Let's take a moment in silence to do this as God longs for nothing more than to love us and for us to love God. Let us draw near to that God now in silence.

Sermon Summary

(The pastor picks up the bread and walks into the congregation.)

Question: What's this?

Answer: Bread

All over the world, right now, there are people who are gathered in much the same situation as this. They are gathered because Jesus gave them a commandment, an instruction, to do something to help them remember him. The symbol he chose was one that was an essential part of their daily lives: bread. Somewhere in the world right now, dressed in a robe made of the finest linen woven fabric, there stands a priest. He holds up a small piece of unleavened bread with the sign of a cross on it. When it is broken and lifted up, bells ring, incense comes out, and light pours through stained glass windows. People draw near and receive a simple piece of bread and wine, doing so because Jesus said, "Every time you eat this bread and drink this cup, do so in remembrance of me."

Somewhere else, just a little bit farther around the world, about forty miles outside of Nairobi, you walk to the end of a dirt road path in the woods leading a village of grass huts. There sit villagers who have heard of God's love. They have taken grain and ground it, mixed it with water, and formed patties that they roast on rocks. On the crude table lay flat little pieces of bread dotted with ash. They have squeezed berries into a wooden bowl to make juice. The elders stand and tell the story about the God who came to earth so that people could have a direct relationship with God. They take one of those bread cakes and break it and they share the juice because Jesus said, "Every time you eat this bread and drink this cup, do so in remembrance of me."

In the center of downtown Hong Kong, surrounded by high-rise sky-scrapers, stands an ordinary-looking building. On one of the floors inside this building is located a sanctuary. Today people will be gathering there, breaking bread and sharing cup in the middle of an enormously populated, secular commerce center. They stand together and say, "Every time you eat this bread and drink this cup, do so in remembrance of me."

Located just around the corner from this building is a park. The park is busy with people selling magazines, candy, and ice cream. On Sunday it becomes strangely vacant, but many women from the Philippines who have come to Hong Kong to be housekeepers gather there. They have Sundays off from work. They gather in this downtown park in the shadows of skyscrapers and sit in parking decks. They share pictures of their families and sit on blankets, telling stories of home. They share their memories. Some of them bring Bibles. Some of the bring guitars. They worship there, separated from family and homeland. There in the Hong Kong forest of skyscrapers they gather to break bread and share the cup because God, who entered flesh long ago said, "You know, every time you eat this bread and drink this cup, remember me."

All over the world the same thing is happening today. Even here, in a relatively new building in the southern portion of the United States, sitting in green padded chairs, there are human beings who speak English in the twenty-first century. There is a person who has very little hair standing in front of them holding a piece of bread. All of them are creatures of God who share the bread because Jesus said, "Every time you eat this bread and drink this cup, remember me."

You are part of a community of faith that is not just here but is stretched all over the world. It stretches back through history and stretches forward into the future. It a community that is built around a memory of God attached to this gift of bread and of cup. A memory of a God who cared enough to slip out of cosmic eternity into temporal reality and to touch people at the point of their brokenness.

I asked you to think about five things that cause you worry, five things that cause you to worry about a loved one, and five things that bring you joy. Now I want you to think about three other things:

How have I acted in such a way as to be untrue to what God has created me to be? How have I sinned . . . *against myself?*

How have I acted in a way that has been untrue to the way God has made me to be *in relationship with others*? Could it be a relationship with your spouse, a friend, a neighbor, someone you just met, or a business associate? How have I sinned in a relationship?

How have I lived my life in such a way as to contribute to the brokenness of the world? Have I participated in prejudice, injustice, or materialism rather than building bridges of attitude or action that strengthen Christian community?

Consider the ways that we have failed to be the people that God has created us to be. We remember our failures not to feel bad about ourselves, but rather to confess them and ask for healing. The Good News is this: If we confess our sins, God is faithful and just, and will forgive our sins, freeing us from all unrighteousness.

Consecration of the Elements

Jesus took bread and gave thanks to God. He thought about how God created the seeds that grew into wheat, and how the wheat was crushed and mixed with other ingredients to make bread. With profound gratitude, he thought about the miracle of God's creation, and the way in which God has lovingly provided for our needs. He broke the bread *(pastor breaks bread)* and said, "This is my Body which is broken for you." He then took the cup *(pours juice)* of shared meals, of weddings, of joy, and of feasts and said, "This cup represents my Blood which is poured out for you. It is the Blood of the new covenant for the forgiveness of sins. Every time you eat this bread and drink this cup, do so in remembrance of me."

Let us take a moment and ask God to forgive us. Let us lift up that which we need to confess in silence knowing that God is here with us. In the name of Jesus Christ, you are forgiven. All of you. In the name of Jesus Christ, you are forgiven. This means you can let go of your worries, of your failures, of your sins. You have been forgiven and you can come to the Table of the Lord.

(Communion servers are invited to come forward.)

Holy Communion

"One Bread, One Body" (UMH 620)

The Offering

Prepare to participate in what God is doing even now in this world.

(In prayer)

Oh, Lord, even before we were born you were active in this world. Even before Abram knew it, you had a destination in mind for him; he trusted you with all that he was and all that he had. Through him and his faithfulness, you have blessed this earth. Oh, Lord, we who stand in that same line, we who long for that same kind of trust and faith, come before you this morning. Out of what you have given to us, we prepare now to offer to you. Lord, help us to see your vision, help us to dream your dreams, help us to be passionately creative and courageous as we allow your work and your will to unfold through us. So bless these gifts and those who would give, that in the act of giving and in the gifts that have been given, your face will be evident in this world and many will know God. In Jesus' name. Amen.

"Light to the Nations" by John Barbour
©1996 Maranatha! Music (Admin. by The Copyright Company)

Closing Music

"The Threads of Our Hearts" *(score included on the DVD)*

The Invitation and Sending Forth

In a world that is often so dark and divided, know that you are light-filled with the One who has called you here. You are called to pour out that light, to illumine the darkness. You are the seasoning, the salt, in a world that is sometimes so bland and flavorless. So as those who are light and salt, prepare now, in peace, to enter the world.

Invitation

As you go out into the world, remember that we are united around this table as brothers and sisters in Christ. We are all children of God. Be messengers and bringers of peace and healers of division. In the name of Jesus, who unites us. Amen.

Appendix 1: Using the DVD

PLAYING THE DVD

ON A SET-TOP PLAYER

Set-top DVD players are connected to a TV. If you have played a DVD motion picture previously, you will see that the *IWS* DVD behaves in much the same way. Once inserted, the disk will begin playing automatically, beginning with the copyright notice and logos. After these have played, the **Main** menu will appear, and you may then use the menu to choose what you would like to view.

To navigate through the DVD menus, use the **Up** and **Down** arrow keys on your remote to move the pointer to the menu item that you wish to play. After an item is highlighted, press **Play** or **Enter** to move to the next screen or to begin playing an item such as a video. Clicking the **Title** button will take you to back to the very beginning of the disk.

Volume is also adjusted in the normal way for your DVD player. Other buttons on the remote, like **Fast Forward,** will allow you to quickly move through a video. Many of the screens also have embedded graphical buttons, such as **Menu,** to help you navigate. Selecting the graphical **Menu** button will take you back one level in the menu structure, depending on where you are. For example, if you have the menu for **Finished Clips** onscreen, selecting **Menu** will take you back one level to the main **Video Clips** menu. To go back to the **Main Menu**, you will need to click the **Title** button on your remote. Selecting the **Back** or **Next** button will move you through the other menus at the same level.

ON A COMPUTER

System Requirements
Windows
- Windows 98 and higher (ME or higher recommended)
- At least 600 MHz processor; 1Ghz or higher recommended
- 128 MB of memory; 256 recommended.
- DVD-ROM drive with appropriate drivers and software

Macintosh

- OS 9 or higher
- G3 processor; 600 Mhz or higher
- At least 128 MB of memory; 256 recommended.
- DVD-ROM drive with appropriate drivers and software

If you have the capability to hook a computer with a DVD player to a projector, you may choose to use this method to display the video components for the services. Every computer will have a different type of proprietary software that comes with the DVD-ROM drive, and the controls on each will vary slightly.

Many of the buttons on the software interface will act just like the buttons on a DVD remote, though there will be some variation. Using the up and down arrow buttons on your software remote will cycle through and highlight each of the buttons, functioning just as they do on a set-top DVD player. (**Up** and **Left** will move through the buttons clockwise; **Down** and **Right** = counter-clockwise.) Once you have highlighted the button you want, hit the **Enter** key to activate the button. The advantage, however, of the computer navigation over the DVD set-top player is your ability to use the mouse to easily select the item you want by clicking it.

In general, clicking the **Menu** button will take you back one step: if you are simply in a menu, it will take you up one level to the previous one; if you are playing a video, it will stop the video and take you back to the sub-menu. You can also use the **Menu** button to exit out of a video and return to the menu. Depending on where you are, you may have several choices when you click the **Menu** button. **Title** takes you back to the very beginning; **Root** takes you back to the previous menu (if this is your only other choice).

Clicking the **Title** button will take you to back to the very beginning of the disk. The **Fast Forward** and **Rewind** buttons will allow you to advance or rewind the video.

ADDITIONAL RESOURCES ON THE DVD

HOW DO I ACCESS THESE RESOURCES?

To access the resources included on the DVD, you will need to place it in a computer DVD-ROM drive. To browse to these data folders in Windows, open **Windows Explorer** and find the **Igniting Worship** disk icon. Double-click the DVD icon for a listing of the contents. (Be patient; it may take several seconds for the list to appear.) You may also use **My Computer** to get a listing of the data folders. However, you will probably need to right-click the DVD icon and choose **Explore** rather than double-clicking since this might cause the DVD to begin playing. On a Macintosh, simply double-click the DVD icon to view the contents of the disk.

Once you have located the file you need, either copy the file to your hard drive or double-click the file to open it from the disk. If you open the file from the disk, remember that manipulating the file this way may be slower than copying it to your hard drive.

Below you will find detailed descriptions of the various types of resources available on the DVD and suggestions for how to use them.

VIDEO CLIPS

Several different types of video clips have been included on the DVD for use in your own worship presentations. These clips have been included as MPEG-1 (.mpg) and MPEG-2 (.m2v) files. The MPEG-1 files are highly compressed and can be easily manipulated and inserted into Microsoft® PowerPoint.® MPEG-2 files are used for professional quality video and is the format used for making DVDs.

MPEG-1 can be viewed in most media players such as Windows® Media Player, Real® Player, and Apple QuickTime® Player. With MPEG-2 files, the video and audio are saved out as separate files. Although players like RealOne Player can play the video portion, it does not play the audio portion (.AC3). You can, however, edit MPEG-2 video in a professional editing package like Adobe® Premiere.®

Finished Clips
These clips combine a number of different scenes related to Communion. Transitions, music beds, and text have been added to create a finished presentation lasting several minutes. These clips may be used as a complete whole.

- **Communion:** These clips contain a montage of images of both the celebration of Communion and the meaning of the elements as they relate to the life, death, and resurrection of Jesus Christ. Two versions of this clip have been provided: one with a traditional music bed and one with a contemporary music bed.

- **Making Bread:** These clips move from scenes of the making of bread in Israel using traditional methods to the image of Jesus as the Bread of Life. Two versions of this clip have been provided: one containing Scriptural text (John 6:35 & 1 Corinthians 5:8) and one without any text.

- **Making Wine/Grape Juice:** These clips begin with scenes showing the processing of grapes into juice and move to images of the Blood of Christ shed for the forgiveness of our sins. Two versions of this clip have been provided: one with a traditional music bed and one with a contemporary music bed.

Rough Clips

These short clips can be customized and combined in your own presentations. Each clip is approximately 30 seconds in length. Using editing software, you can combine these clips into your own customized video or simply use one of the clips as a brief illustration in a presentation. These clips are:

- Group of young adults serving one another Communion
- Minister saying the Words of Institution
- Communion in a Hispanic church
- Communion in a Korean church
- Volunteers preparing Communion trays
- Individuals kneeling at the altar in prayer during Communion
- Children receiving Communion

Illustrative Clips

These clips have been provided by the church authoring this volume of the *Igniting Worship Series* and contain footage from actual worship celebrations. They have been included primarily to illustrate how particular elements in the corresponding worship services were handled.

- **Coming Home for Communion** (Service 1): Images and explanation of the Communion Table as the place where Christians come together as the family of God.

- **The Body of Christ in Action** (Service 6): Scenes of congregation preparing mission relief bags.

- **Communion Through the Eyes of a Child** (Service 7): Scenes of children making bread for Communion.

- **Walking Today Where Jesus Walked** (Service 9): Scenes from an original drama depicting the events of Holy Week (included in the service).

Permissions

You may use these video clips only in the context of a worship service, provided you include the following acknowledgment in your presentation:

Video clip from *Igniting Worship: Communion, by Grace Community Church and SpiritFilms*™ © 2003 Abingdon Press. Used by permission.

MUSIC SCORES

Music scores for three original songs by Stacy Hood have been included on the DVD as PDF files (in the folder named **IWS Communion Music Scores**). To open these files, you will need to have Adobe© Acrobat© Reader installed on your computer. You can obtain this free software download from www.adobe.com/acrobat.) Once you have opened the file, you may print it using the **Print** icon on the Acrobat Reader toolbar. Songs included are:

- "Can We Drink This Cup?" (Service 8)
- "Remember Me" (Service 9)
- "The Threads of Our Hearts" (Service 10)

WORSHIP BACKGROUNDS

Coordinating worship backgrounds for each service have been included on the DVD in the folder, **IWS Communion Worship Backgrounds**. Each set contains three graphic images, in both BMP and JPEG formats. Together they will provide the basic needs for an integrated worship experience. Below is a brief explanation of each type and suggestions for how to use them:

Main Image

The main image contains the title of the particular service, and can be displayed throughout your worship experience. Think of it as a default title image that can fill the visual "holes" in worship, rather than having a blank screen. This main image can also be used to provide smooth transitions between elements in worship. For example, when the call to worship has finished and the musicians are on their way to their instruments, you could put the graphic up to divert your congregation's attention away from the setup and keep it focused on the worship experience as this transition takes place.

Song Background

On the song background, a portion of the main image has been blurred so that text placed over can be easily read. You may use this background for song lyrics, Scriptures, responsive prayers, and anything else containing more than a couple of lines of text.

Main Image With No Words

This image has been included so that you can add your own custom sermon points, as well as any additional illustrations that you may have. If you have quite a bit of text to put over the image (like a Scripture verse), you should use the song background.

Appendix 2: Church Video License

Movies and movies clips are marvelous ways to illustrate Scripture with contemporary images and parables. It is vital that church leaders use these materials legally. Even more important are the ethical and moral responsibilities of the church to be certain that artists who produce these materials are fairly compensated. A CVLI license to cover use of videos produced "for home use only" will help ensure this.

THE LAW—The U.S. Copyright Act of 1976 gives copyright owners almost total control of the use of their copyrighted works. Pre-recorded videocassettes and DVDs are released—*For-Home Use Only*—unless you have permission to show them in public. Without permission, you may be subject to substantial penalties.

WHO IS CVLI?

CVLI is a partnership between Motion Picture Licensing Corporation (MPLC) and Christian Copyright Licensing International (CCLI). It focuses on the educational and entertainment needs of the religious community.

RELIGIOUS INSTITUTIONS CAN GET PERMISSION—Religious institutions can show videos and be in accordance with the U.S. Copyright Act by using one of the following methods:

1. Show videos which have "Public Performance Rights,"

2. Attempt to receive written permission prior to the use of the video and pay the copyright holder directly, or

3. Obtain coverage with the Church Video license from CVLI.

The license covers the widest variety of titles ranging from faith-based and family values videos to major Hollywood features.

WHAT IS A VIDEO LICENSE?

Through an agreement with more than 70 Hollywood studios and Christian producers, your church license provides legal coverage to show an unlimited number of home videos and DVDs of motion pictures at a variety of your church's functions and activities. You can show full-length films at church programs or clips at worship services. A license for additional programs within the ministry such as daycare facilities, schools, camps, and conference centers are available for an additional fee.

The license does not cover materials that have been copied from another source or recorded from television. It also does not allow charging admission fees or advertising or publicizing specific titles in local media.

Beginning next year, ScreenVue, a company affiliated with CVLI, will also offer selections of film clips to illustrate Scripture and Christian character-related topics on a subscription basis to all licensees.

QUESTIONS AND ANSWERS

Q. *We own the video, do we still need a license to view or show it in public?*

A. Yes. The location requires a license regardless of who owns the cassette or DVD. While you may own the actual cassette or DVD, you are only granted the right to view it in your home, not to perform it in public.

Q. *We do not charge admission. Do we still need a license?*

A. Yes. The U.S. Copyright Act states that regardless of whether an admission fee is charged, a license is required. In fact, the Church Video License does not cover showings where an admission fee is charged.

Q. *We are non-profit. Do we still need a license?*

A. Yes. The legal requirement to obtain a license applies equally to non-profit and for-profit organizations.

Q. *How much does a Church Video License cost?*

A. License fees are affordable and are based on the size of your membership.

Q. *We are a Sunday school or child care center, do we qualify for a "face-to-face" teaching exemption?*

A. No. The educational exemption is narrowly defined and applies to full-time, non-profit academic institutions only.

Q. *We are not open to the general public. Do we still need a license?*

A. Yes. Any location outside of the home is considered public for copyright purposes.

Q. *We sometimes make our facilities available to other groups. Who is liable for copyright infringement?*

A. The exhibitor is considered the "primary infringer," but where the owner is in the position to control conduct of the "primary infringer," he may be held vicariously liable or considered a "contributory infringer."

Obtaining a CVLI License

The licensing procedure is easy. Contact CVLI toll-free at **(888) 302-6020** or United Methodist Communications at **(888) 346-3862**. For a list of producers included in the CVLI license, consult the CVLI website (www.cvli.org). This list is updated regularly.

Appendix 3: List of the Video Clips Included on the DVD

Finished Clips

- **Communion:** This clip contains a montage of images of both the celebration of Communion and the meaning of the elements as they relate to the life, death, and resurrection of Jesus Christ. Two versions of this clip have been provided: one with a traditional music bed and one with a contemporary music bed.

  Keywords: *Bread, wine, grapes, grape juice, cup, chalice, loaf, Jesus, crucifixion, passion, crown of thorns, cross, nails, Last Supper, Korean, Hispanic, minister, prayer, intinction, Words of Institution ("This is my body...").*

- **Making Bread:** This clips moves from scenes of the making of bread in the Israel using traditional methods to the image of Jesus as the Bread of Life. Two versions of this clip have been provided: one containing Scriptural text (John 6:35 & 1 Corinthians 5:8), and one without any text.

  Keywords: *Bread, oven, fire, baking, dough, Israel, leaven, John 6:35, 1 Corinthians 5:8, hands, kneading, "Bread of Life."*

- **Making Wine/Grape Juice:** This clip begins with the scenes from a vineyard showing the process of making wine and moves to images of the Blood of Christ shed for the forgiveness of our sins. Two versions of this clip have been provided: one with a traditional music bed and one with a contemporary music bed.

  Keywords: *Grapes, vines, juice, chalice, Blood of Christ.*

Rough Clips
- Group of young adults serving one another Communion
- Minister saying the Words of Institution
- Communion in a Hispanic church
- Communion in a Korean church
- Volunteers preparing Communion trays
- Individuals kneeling at the altar in prayer during Communion
- Children receiving Communion

Additional Resources from Grace Community Church

ReConnecting:
A Wesleyan Guide for the Renewal of Our Congregation
By Rob Weber

ReConnecting is a seven-week or seven-session experience designed to help your congregation reconnect with some of the major themes and principles in the ministry of John Wesley. However, this experience does not simply provide a lesson in Wesleyan history or theology. These themes and principles are applicable to all churches and all generations, and their recovery is meant to transform and re-energize the journey of discipleship on both the personal and corporate level. *ReConnecting* may be customized and used in a variety of settings—as an adult Lenten study, as a renewal program, or as a study of Wesleyan heritage.

Leader's Guide with DVD
ISBN: 0-687-02234-7
Price: $39.00

Participant's Guide (Does not include DVD)
ISBN: 0-687-06535-6

Included on DVD that comes with Leader's Guide:
* Leader's Guide included on DVD as a PDF file (printed book contains text of the Participant's Guide)
* Promotional Video Trailer (a summary of the sessions).
* Customizable Poster (TIFF and PDF formats)
* Publicity material (Sample letters, brochure, and registration card).

System Requirements:

DVD is compatible with most DVD set top players and computer DVD-ROM players.

Visual Leadership:
The Church Leader As ImageSmith
By Rob Weber

Weber stresses the importance for a church leader in our current multisensory and multicultural society to lead through engaging people in the multisensory world of images. This kind of leadership requires skills in storytelling and media. The leader must develop sensitivity to a variety of media forms as well as an understanding of the multiple levels of story and the images out of which (and into which) people live.

ISBN: 0-687-07844-X Paper, $15.00

ReKindling:
A Guide for Congregations with Multiple Or Alternative Worship Patterns
By Stacy Hood

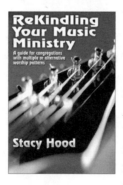

Whether your church is looking to add to a traditional music program or start a nontraditional music ministry, *ReKindling Your Music Ministry* provides worship leaders advice on making an effective transition into a new music format by reducing or better managing conflict. The "key" ingredient in a music ministry is to focus hearts on doing God's will-which is an excellent antidote to anxieties about entertain-ment and performance in worship.

ISBN: 0-687-04421-9 Paper, $15.00
(Also available as an eBook)